Was and Is: Collected Poems

Neil Powell was born in London in 1948 and educated at Sevenoaks School and the University of Warwick. He has taught English, owned a bookshop and, since 1990, been a full-time author and editor. His books include seven previous collections of poetry – of which the most recent is *Proof of Identity* (2012) – as well as *Carpenters of Light* (1979), *Roy Fuller: Writer and Society* (1995), *The Language of Jazz* (1997), *George Crabbe: An English Life* (2004), *Amis & Son: Two Literary Generations* (2008) and *Benjamin Britten: A Life for Music* (2013). He lives in Suffolk.

Also by Neil Powell

At the Edge
Carpenters of Light
A Season of Calm Weather
True Colours
The Stones on Thorpeness Beach
Roy Fuller: Writer and Society
The Language of Jazz
Selected Poems
George Crabbe: An English Life
A Halfway House
Amis & Son: Two Literary Generations
Proof of Identity
Benjamin Britten: A Life for Music

NEIL POWELL

Was and Is
Collected Poems

CARCANET

First published in Great Britain in 2017 by
Carcanet Press Ltd
Alliance House, 30 Cross Street
Manchester M2 7AQ
www.carcanet.co.uk

A CIP catalogue record for this book is available from the British Library.
ISBN 9781784102326

Typeset by XL Publishing Services, Exmouth

The publisher acknowledges financial assistance
from Arts Council England.

Supported using public funding by
**ARTS COUNCIL
ENGLAND**

For absent friends:
Matthew, Adam and Rod

Contents

II   *1976–1986*

III *1987–1997*

IV *1998–2011*

Preface

There are two ways of doing a *Collected Poems*. One suits authors whose poems have previously appeared as a neat sequence of coherent slim volumes and are not to be disturbed by reordering or revising. This is the other sort.

I've attempted to arrange the poems as far as possible in order of composition or at least completion; the exceptions are the various sequences, some of which have components written months or even years apart and which therefore have to be placed, a little more subjectively, where they most appropriately fit. I've deleted a handful of previously published poems which I no longer like, for one reason or another, and inserted a slightly larger handful of unpublished pieces which I seem to have overlooked in the past. Otherwise, my revisions have been mainly confined to corrections of misprints, sense or syntax; I've also amended a faulty rhyme scheme in one case and, in another, a miscounted syllabic line. A *Collected Poems* is not quite the same thing as a *Complete Poems*: a box file with the latter label contains a vast amount of other material, mostly juvenilia, for my hapless literary executor to discover one day.

Michael Schmidt at Carcanet has been my poetry publisher since I appeared in his anthology *Ten English Poets* in 1976; my first collection, *At the Edge*, followed in 1977. I don't quite know how we've put up with each other for all these years nor what I – and an astonishing range of other contemporary poets – would have done without him.

N.P.

I
1966–1975

A Black Cat in July

Tuesday morning. The ground is bright wet,
the sky fixed, static, the cloud not yet
broken. After breakfast I walked too
far, for I had forgotten that you
might be here, and I am overtired:
thoughts desert me when they are required.

Not that I believe in witchcraft or
whatever else black cats are used for;
naturally, I laugh at the idea,
yet somehow, unnaturally, fear
the outcome of my ignoring you,
lurking among the leaves, brushed with dew.

Premonitions read in black-green eyes
I nervously dismiss as the lies
of imagination. But what glows
there, what strange unknown prophecy grows
in this darkness? Some quiet strength steers
our fate, through too many hollow tears,

finding paths among the falling years.

Wickham Market

The smell and feel of leather fill the bar.
The farmers fake oblivion, or else stare
Resentment, looks more weatherbeaten than
The invader's crumpled armour. There the rain
Has streaked a relic of some recent battle,
Evidence that elements are more brittle

Than his shell. And yet he stands rain-scarred,
His hair is limp, and his rough cheeks are teared
From the storm still raging in his eyes:
Possessing and possessed, they half-despise
Their ambiguity, for they gleam that
Quick self-knowledge which will never let
Him be touched, though it will bid all try,
Reflecting all, a mirror to each lie –
The tragic clown. He turns towards his friend,
Buys him a drink, and laughs, sensing the end
Of the last storm is also the beginning
Of the next, that loss is in his winning.

Solstice

The sun is pausing. Now reflected

in this pond are winter's images,
a barren tree and one or two dead
leaves adrift in time's dark passages.

The branches gather round us. Pausing,
we look for moorhens and see, crusted
on the banks, a dead year, a rippling

premonition of frost. Clinging, we
try to find warmth, but we too have paused
at this season's apex. Just now the

sound of spring seemed present in the dregs
of the year; I know now that I heard
merely the snapping of winter twigs.

Five Leaves Left

1

It is winter.

On a beech tree
by my window
I see five leaves hanging.

Listen to them falling.

2

The bird morning
loud then terrible
grew. And I knew

the trees had changed.

It was the bird
morning I wrote
some white word
on a wall, knowing
almost all. The word

has no meaning.

In that momentary pride,
the heart of summer died.

3

No, I am no tree. If
I were, I would have
fallen. My roots are
hacked about, and where
they still remain secure,
people stand: stay there.

4

There was always snow.

Always, slow dropping
in the receding night,
and you awoke. The world gleaming,
older now.

And colder as time
fell thickly on the flame.

Only evening skies were red.

5

The silent sky
shone sullen through
a stained-glass window.

Light, colour, the
purple and bronze,
words cloaked deep
in gold, vague shapes
yet precise feelings.

These colours breathe
a benediction.

6

And one deeper mystery.

The cold damp evening,
the mist lingering
among the hills. No
colour, only the slow
now faster heartbeat.
Only now you forget
beat, know only that
you know.

7

The leaves fall faster
than you think. The tree
is bare. And so, later

than I had thought, am I.

And it is winter.

For My Ancestors

All summer long, I listened:
hearing the river ripple
in the shallows of my brain,

before winter, and the floods,
and the giant boughs floating
downstream in the wake of rain.

Then I walked beneath night skies,
hearing no birds, among the
tombstones, the spire's black outline

above me, and thought of those
buried there, and almost for
a moment wished to see a sign

of my own past engraved on
some decrepit, crumbling stone.
I wondered what sort of men

my ancestors might have been:
if they fought for their country,
or for themselves, or if (when

they heard horses' hooves, gunfire
or shouts) they hid among trees
and tried to make some pattern

from the leaves. If they did, then
I have inherited their
fear, solitude, and even

a little of their talent;
for I too must always hear
twigs snapping, the river run,

and the sound of evening birds.

At Berkswell

for John & Hilary Sutton

Awaiting us, it hides, a place apart.

The village shops, the school, the almshouses
Surround it like a cold grey congregation
Who once knew how to pray, and watch in case
The place's vital essence should escape.
Proximity invites us to survey
The church's quiet order and decay.

A timbered Tudor porch stands to our right,
Incongruously welded to the flat
Substantial Norman wall: no one in sight
Except a sexton and a resident cat.
Inside, we look around, begin to know
How little changes where few people go.

Tradition too secure for sentiment
Is here encased in timber, stone and glass,
To demonstrate that our predicament
Is unimportant. Years and tourists pass.
It waits behind here, watching us depart.
Forgetting us, it hides, a place apart.

Identities

He thinks he knows a little about love.
A river-bank, the branches crowding round,
Imprisoning the sun, the yellow leaves
Embracing, wilting slightly in the heat;
Those stream-smooth pebbles, lying just too deep
To reach. The sound of water in the hills,
A vacant summer evening closing in,
The darkening grass, the branches vanishing.
Watching his mirror-image watching him
Behind the bar, he almost loves himself.

Almost. And yet his mind is following
A cloud across a birdless winter sky,
Or prints set hard in snow, or passages
Through leafless woods. The geometric trees
Do not embrace: they touch, scratch and unfold
The wounds of winter, the futility
Of making contact. Best to stand and drink
Secure in some bright apathetic world;
To wait, and hope someone will penetrate
His abstract code, but still not understand.

It is an old accepted paradox,
Escape's vague border with reality.
He needs a bar, an image and a pose
To which the moss of solitude will cling.
He turns and says, 'The counterpoint of Bach
Is like that of the Modern Jazz Quartet
But not so brittle.' Living in an age
Of jagged noises and too brittle sounds,
We choose either the wilted summer leaf
Or else the branches' patterned skeleton.

He thinks of blind men, tries to share the lack
Of image crushed upon the retina:
They have their perfect vision, not the sight
Of years or days or placid winter skies;
Yet he retains the fading vestiges,
The summers and the fallings out of love.
He chooses winter, treading where the fox
Has trod, where rabbits ran some other day,
And where the tracks are frozen hard. He thinks
He knows too little and too much of love.

Previous Convictions

1

Whether it snowed much that winter is unimportant:
        it was a beginning and as such, chiefly,
I shall remember it. The bar we sat in was brown-
        painted: a gas fire spluttered irritably
in one corner, the landlord in another; Christmas
        loomed, a conventional iceberg, easily
navigated. Season of booze and Bach: each evening
        we listened to cheap records, drew from the sound
of a flautist's drastic breathing and the impatient
        scrape of furious 'cellos a deeper strand
of pleasure than from more perfect art.
                                        Or that at least
        was how it seemed, or seems now: the imperfections
necessary evidence of a humanity
        certain to disappear at any moment,
lost in the immaculate circle at the centre
        of the record. The intransigence of sound,
which at its most intimate keeps its distance, held us
        close and apart. We cannot talk of music,

we can only listen: the academic, given
        to confusing criticism with the art
it preys on, finds in it pleasure and perplexity;
        for print does not contain it, nor notation
yield the essence of its mystery.
                                And, driving back
        from some lonely pub, deep among the frosty
hopfields, we bounced from side to side of a steep-banked lane,
        while the Irishman on the back seat hardly
stopped talking, and claimed afterwards not to have noticed.
        There, buried in the night and in the country,
we devised ideas of life and friendship, to ripen
        through summer and be crushed like fallen berries
in the autumn. Their stains remain, more permanent than those
        of ordinary fruit.
                        Like grey prophecies,
multiplying smoke strata hung in that vaulted room,
        long after music had ended and bottles
were empty. The sound of the rain increases slowly,
        and the smoke begins to settle into dust.

2

        And winter's light, the sharp
        separating of the branches,
        filled with certain uncertainties,
        comes again,
                        solves no problems:

        suicide or emigration
        are paltry gestures, mean replies
        to some ungenerous invitation.

3 ('The ethics of return …')

South again. The loyalties of home
Make, quietly, their comfortable claims.
Half-wilfully mistaken, they presume
To know what happened elsewhere, or in dreams;

Or in confusion wilfully confuse
The alienated voice with the obscure.
I use the vocabulary I use,
But seldom ask that anyone should hear.

4

For, yes, you have heard it all before:
An old familiar tune you too once sang
In another key has now become a chant
Whispered in half-light, under falling night.

Antique bronze leaves are not surprising now,
But evidence of what we dread to see:
An earthquake in the floorboards springs within;
Beneath lead skies, an outer fire dies.

The old nostalgia! Thus again today
I looked through pine trees at a dying sun
And saw, at this late season, how we grow
Not up, but downwards, into deepening snow.

The Window

Emptiest moment of night:
As the streetlamp outside
Clicks off and invisible rain
Drums out a dull platitude,
An endless monotonous tune,
And no voice whispers *write*.

Books on the shelves proclaim
Their own existences:
Having nothing to do with me,
They keep their distances,
Compelling me to see
For this I'm alone to blame.

Believing is the act
We try to play by day
To mock the midnight void.
But charged by memory,
Whom we ourselves employed,
And who will not retract

In the court of self-esteem,
We have no advocate,
And find the sentence tough:
We are not ourselves, and yet
There is no one we like enough
To wish to be like them.

It is no more than the mime
Of a greedy, hungry age:
We act it or else fail
In either greed or courage,
Admitting there is no rule,
No energy, no time.

Yet the cycle has begun:
Veering from despair,
From pedantry, avarice,
Or Arnold's damp night air,
And full of helpful advice,
I wish I had a son.

After Marriage

A girl when you married; now,
at twenty, a woman and
fallen out of love. Of course,
a Spanish gypsy warned you
and (you knew) was right. Because
you have known most answers most
questions are superfluous.

Most, not all. This long winter
has frozen your mask too hard;
thawing, it silently cracks,
and the anecdotes admit
a desperate nostalgia:
life's problems undefeated
but, defeated, life itself.

Or mastered perhaps: precise
distinction between coolness
and cynicism defeats
us, confusion our habit
and cloister. We seek at best
some finer limitation:
an act and the strength of trust.

'Autumn is the curse of English poetry'

I watch the wet leaves gather in the gutter
And, on my desk, a sympathetic clutter.

★

At dusk, the strident solitary bird:
All poets know this, but how few have heard.

★

To read Hardy in the autumn sets a context
(Waking from one dream, we enact the next).

★

How well the mellow elegiac tone
Suits summer's fleshy corpse, which has no bone.

★

The word makes up for what the weather lacks,
And language obeys the seasons' syntax.

The Cricketers

From the woodland's edge I watched the cricketers,
Their casual dedication and their clear
Instinct of movement's boundaries. It was
The time of evening when the gnats appear.

Not far away, the bracken shrieked and moved:
The boy was asking if she really cared
When she got up to go; he watched, unloved.
Neither was beautiful nor, it seemed, prepared.

They left the wood. Then, hearing from behind
That curiously unresonant applause,
I turned towards the cricket-pitch to find
The cricketers had disappeared indoors.

It was no more than proof of finitude,
An artifice enclosed by space and time:
For game as well as poem must exclude
All but the chosen number, stress, or rhyme.

We seek these limits, ordered and controlled,
Unlike the gracelessness of doubtful lovers:
A world confined within the poem's mould
Or circumscribed by boundaries and overs;

Though, thinking this, I find myself clean bowled.

Wood Farm

Clutching this twisted rusty
key, like some furtive gaoler,
I find the back door. Slowly,
the lock unsticks. I enter,
glancing quickly round although
only nettles live here now.

This place lacks the old-house smell
of rotting timber, other
autumns' leaves, and the quick fall
of crumbling plaster. I stare
across the ochre air, drawn
to interminable brown.

The beams creak; the rain gently
taps on a cracked window-pane;
and outside the falling grey
East Anglian afternoon
turns silently to evening
as I wait here wondering

about our pasts and futures.
Farmers prospered here: their food
graced this oven; their pastures,
lands made heavy with their blood,
are barren now; the soil grows
mere scrub, dead with its owners.

And dead for the future too.
Rest in peace. Let the poppies
colour this place and the dew
shine on the shattered windows,
reflecting through slow decay
a natural dignity.

A Modern Jazz Quartet

Duke Ellington

Modern? Of course: *Ulysses*
and *The Waste Land* were written
long before *Mood Indigo*.

Though at ease with a keyboard,
pen rather than piano
is your chosen instrument,

the writer's craft replacing
performer's pyrotechnics
in the study's sanctuary:

a poet, substituting
orchestra for typewriter.
I wish I knew the language.

Charlie Parker

Time has distilled these moments,
has sanctified place and date:
Los Angeles, '48,

the point at which suffering
and expertise intersect
in a blues called *Parker's Mood*.

A secret, mysterious
music of purity and
uncanny classicism:

it is clearer now because
unrivalled and unsurpassed,
distilled through a sense of time.

Thelonious Monk

During a tenor solo
at the Royal Festival Hall
you stood up and blew your nose.

The gesture was typical,
the solo was very dull,
and most of us got the point.

So, typically, you find
a perfect absurdity
in the cracks between the keys;

for reverence is no use
to a music which rejects
the gloss of solemnity.

John Coltrane

You managed the paradox:
out of certainty you brought
the music of confusion.

Through commitment you had seen
that tone does not carry truth:
one must travel in-between.

There is no perfection here
for each new cluster of notes
diminishes certainty.

One would not have guessed your creed
could be so painfully wrought
into such complexity.

The Ruined Garden

These are the foundations. Roots of walls
Map out the careful pattern of a home.
The great house seems so curiously small.

The south view is magnificent: the downs
Merge gently into mist, if you could see.
Now giant rhododendrons block the light
And blossom at the unresponsive sky.

Round the great lawn, ornamental trees
Have overreached themselves. A colony
Of rooks invades the intermingled boughs,
Applauds a ruined aristocracy.

Wealth and Empire, bland extravagance,
The wasteful whims and pleasures of the rich:
These are the foundations.

A Midsummer Letter to Peter Thornton

The evening has turned thundery. The lamp
Is switched on several hours before dusk:
The artificial light upon the page
Induces strident artificial words.
This summer is already overtired:
The air sweats; even early morning leaves
Are dusty, dry and derelict. It seems
Some transcendental fan has been turned off
And we are caught between its slowing blades,
Revolving on a dying impetus,
Unmotivated, almost without life.

Briefly, my location. If you drive
North out of Oxford on the Stratford road
And past the barren airport, gradually
The scenery gets better. Through Woodstock
(Which is at least discreetly tarted up)
The road begins to rise, the landscape starts
To look like landscape, not just bits of stone
And ragged vegetation. Woodlands thicken,
Fenced in by those aggressive notices
Which don't just say *Keep Out* but which imply
That lucky trespassers will be arrested,
Unlucky ones more likely shot or lynched.
Then to Enstone, seedy half-spoilt village,
The gloomiest hotel in Oxfordshire,
And after that the road goes up again
Onto the Cotswolds' bleak solidity.
At last some promise: crumbling dry stone walls,
A ruined barn or two, a sense of space,
Proximity to earth and to the sky.
Four miles on, a turning to the left
Leads to this gaunt unfriendly market town.
The square is good, severe and functional
And mostly Cotswold stone; the splendid church
Stands half-concealed, apart, surrounded by
A labyrinth of alleyways and lanes.
The charm ends there. The rambling ornate store
Which graced a corner of the market place
Is now a heap of timber, stone and dust;
The Unicorn next door is falling down,
Its windows glassless, crippled beams exposed;
Across the road an elegant façade
Becomes another neon supermarket
(As a concession to our heritage,
The upper storeys will remain intact,
Or seem so from the road, they say. So much
For culture, conservation and our taste.)

It's not the change alone that worries me,
It's the exchange. The demolition's fine,
So long as something's going in its place:
But nothing is. That supermarket too:
Are we so very short of confidence
That gracious outward trappings must become
A specious and redundant artifice
Made ludicrous by what goes on below?

The climate's changed. It isn't merely thunder
But the insistent climate of the mind:
The ways that deaths affect us as perhaps
A symptom or a barometric truth.
Forster died last month, then Allen Lane –
Liberal writer, liberal publisher –
They go together, and now both are gone.
They were the climate which gave confidence
That civilisation wasn't just a ghost,
A musty phantom in some library.
Or myth invented by the BBC
And advertised in Sunday supplements.
They were the climate into which we grew.

Now Democratic Man has slipped again:
That amiable and aimless animal
Who thinks Brand X is best and who mistakes
His dreams of cash for grander dreams of change.
Politics, his favourite rocking-chair,
Rocks back again: five years of juggling
With business sense and cold efficiency
Will follow on five years of human error.
We will of course be 'better off': that is,
The figures will declare our affluence,
The Stock Exchange will be more 'confident',
Our ethics will be cosily forgotten.
No doubt South Africa will buy our arms,
Trade will pick up, the flow of cash increase,

And the worst instincts of Competitive Man
Will flower and then bear their brazen fruit.
To them it looks like progress, to me death.

I almost envy you outside it all
In philistine Australia. At least
You know the score and, knowing it, escape
The vicious whirlpool which must draw us in
And down upon ourselves. Stability,
The goal pursued by every right-wing state,
Is necessarily The Australian Dream:
That hard stability – which is to say
A total lack of movement – is the thing
I fear most. So I almost envy you,
But finally prefer the English flux,
And hope that flux will reassert itself
Before we turn to monuments of ice.

Inertia's in the climate. It comes on
Insidiously as sleep in afternoon:
That waking sleep through which we speculate
On schemes and patterns, ludicrous ideas
Or trivial pleasures never realised –
A potent and an anaesthetic power,
Leaving sour contentment, a bad head,
And craving for a drink at opening time.
How to resist it, how to organise
Our thoughts into our actions, that's the problem:
How to discern a structure which supplies
The necessary strength as well as form.
A style is not enough. The stoic stance,
For all its good intentions and its charm,
Can only reinforce the circumstance:
Inertia is the end of all endurance.

Distons Lane

for Ian Smith

I'm still a stranger here. As I approach,
A woman crosses to the other side,
Suspicious and afraid that I encroach
On her town's secret privacy or pride.
I understand I am not understood.

I do encroach. I see what's beautiful
In these stark cottages of yellow stone:
The bleakness and the silence of it all.
She sees a grimy terrace, cold, run-down:
A dead-end street, the dead end of the town.

She's known this town too long to be amazed
By filtered sunlight seeping to her yard:
Stone-coloured light, diffusing as she gazed
Into the bronze, stone-mellow and stone-hard.
I understand I am not understood.

She's seen some changes. Her young husband fought
In the Great War, if not the other one
Before it. Now she guards her past in thought:
The cobbles covered, all the gaslamps gone,
A dead-end street, the dead end of the town.

She passes me and glances back in fear,
A shrinking face within an old grey hood.
I smile and know I'm still a stranger here.
'It is not, nor it cannot come to good?'
I understand I am not understood.

Period Three

I stop before the door, compose myself,
Then enter slowly. Certain faces turn
To contemplate my manner or my tie;
A few glance quickly, anxious now to learn
What Wordsworth really meant, and instantly.
I look around for signs of coming storms,
And swiftly launch into the holy life
Of music and of verse and UCCA forms.

The wind is rising: halfway through Book One,
The man's done nothing but apologise
For not quite being Milton; even worse,
His idle boasts and foolish prophecies
Are fossilised in blank and turgid verse.
I answer; and the correspondent breeze
Picks up my notes and elsewhere sets them down.
I stare into the unwordsworthian trees,

And know, however dimly, I am right
To proffer in this heavy autumn room
The relevance of all those thinking things
To all these thinking people. Through the gloom
Of apathy, a voice speaks, a bell rings;
Outside the open window, others shout.
The half-extinguished visionary light
Abruptly and annoyingly goes out.

So, irritated rather than perplexed,
I gather up my notes; now from behind,
A thoughtful voice asks, *Could I have a word?*
I tell him, *Yes, of course: what's on your mind?*
And as he speaks I realise he's heard
It all. He's not the brightest of the class,
But he has seen a poem not a text,
And understood, although he may not pass.

I wander down the corridor, my pace
Too evidently lacking urgency;
A colleague says good morning and I stare
Past him into the dark immobile sky –
That loony poet bloke. I need some air,
But steel myself to teach another bunch.
I stop before the door, prepare to face
Another forty minutes before lunch.

A Pebble

A pebble vanishes. I watch the ripples
Fatten like folds in grey concentric flesh.

The bristling reeds entangle and distort
Those outer circles. River banks enmesh

The insubstantial currents of the mind,
Whose streams contend with assonance and stress.

The poem's flow – the rock pools or the bends,
Metre or syntax, shaping its slow progress –

Becomes a formal fountain as we turn
Our private art to public artifice;

And pebbles dropping softly from a bridge
Are caught within a cave of brittle ice.

Afternoon Dawn

for Rod Shand

They are felling the dead elms
to the west: the sidelong sun
surprises the room after
a hundred years of shadow.
The forgotten web and dust
on untouched books are sunstruck.
Clearly, something has begun.

Things that had been unspecial
are transmogrified, reborn
to *duende* and charisma.
Sun settles on faded spines;
crystals through a decanter;
chases spiders in this, its
perversely afternoon dawn;

lights upon Márquez: *through the*
window they saw a light rain
of tiny yellow flowers
falling. Through the window I
see a blue haze of woodsmoke
spiralling towards evening,
hovering, rising again.

The room begins to darken;
now, blood-coloured light splashes
across the page where the pen
labours towards conclusion.
An end to the beginning,
the web once more unnoticed;
the elms will soon be ashes.

Gathering

for John Mole and Peter Scupham

The waiting audience wears its poetry face,
Expectant and defensive. This great room
Seems cavernous, a more than empty space.

You look around, take stock. Can you assume
Some interest, involvement? Maybe not:
The shades of philistines lurk in the gloom.

You banish them. Their insubstantial plot
Melts in mere breath, unutterably reversed
By utterance unscarred by blur or blot.

The poem slowly written, long rehearsed,
Imposes its own pattern, carefully:
Your prodigy, as often loved as cursed.

We mitigate our given destiny
By trying to contain it; thus we trace
Between regard and curiosity

The narrow line which hovers in this place,
Encounter not art's seedlings but its bloom
And gather, pricelessly, some part of grace.

At Little Gidding

for Matthew Desmond

1

In one hand Eliot, in the other Pevsner:
And yet we have arrived here unprepared.

2

Outside the farmhouse, a removal van
Announces a more permanent arrival:
Those clean cream walls seem inappropriate;
New settlers upset the visitor.

3

But not the church, which has seen worse than this:
Scrubby bushes, grey pock-marked façade
Proclaim a calm more honest and more modest,
God's domesticity.

4

The scale is human.
Thus, quizzically, you rightly say you find
The tombstones more impressive than the church.
Grandeur was never Nicholas Ferrar's style;
His, the potent blend of craft and creed.

5

Not that this is Nicholas Ferrar's church.
It is his spirit's church; his church's spirit
Inhabits the carved ceiling of the chancel,
Informs the space beneath.

6

                                    We sign the book.
Something you had not guessed had yet begun
Is completed in this ritual: the place
Belongs to us now; we are part of it.

7

Lifesize, it will stay with us as token
Of the size a life should be: it questions,
And Pevsner's words, not Eliot's, reply,
'Little Gidding is a confusing church.'

8

Only respect transcends confusion. Yes,
In the end, we were impressed. Deliberately,
We close the door, for birds are troublesome
(A notice tells us) and this church is loved.

9

Leighton Bromswold: 'Wonderful,' says Pevsner;
But we have no taste for it today.

The Key

You offered me the key. I saw
How shrewdly it was cut, how well
The cunning craftsman knew the door
It would control: I saw it all.
You should have offered it before.

The patterns forged in steel or rock
By smith or sculptor have no grace,
Mere remnants of the solid block
Until they fill a chosen space.
You should have given me the lock.

In the Distance

First, the foreground. A class is reading,
Gratefully engrossed and undisturbed
By coughs or scraping metal chairs on wood.
Now is a time to watch unwatched, observe
The chin upon the wrist, the narrowed eyes,
The stifled yawn, the silence; and outside
An autumn bonfire flaring in the distance.

Consider this October close-up: hands
Clasped after the cold in new discovery
Of each other's throbbing warmth; a pen
Composing doodles no one understands;
A briefly broken train of thought; and then
The meditative meeting, nose with thumb.
Mist is blurring the horizon distantly.

The years are misting over. I recall
Something I didn't say a dream ago,
Return abruptly to the reading class.
The weeping condensation on a window
Becomes the image of another day,
A conversation in a different place
Minutely glimpsed, and very far away.

What casual things define me! Clothes I wear,
Books I carry, a ballpoint on the desk
Upon a half-corrected essay: there
Is all the life I seem to have. The trees
Branch from the mist, their structures become clear;
The bonfire flashes sharply as I stare
Across a hundred yards, a dozen years.

In the distance, on a Kentish hillside,
A boy is writing a poem I know by heart.

Kimbolton, 1973

The head is from Masaccio – St John –
And he may earn that tribute: parson's son,
He wears a wistful crucifix which glows
Over his leather jacket. What he knows
He does not say: his silences contain
A particle of wisdom, some disdain,
And the discretion of a single mind.
He drinks here often, though it's not his kind
Of pub: fake beams and plastic-covered stools
Set up reflections of a world of fools
In which it pays to play the stranger – strange
To see him count his minutes and his change.
From Wickham Market, seven years away,

Things haven't altered much: only the day
Has darkened to a clear December night
Through winter's sharply analytic light.
Those seven years ago, a coin was tossed.
They took the world away. The winner lost.

Midwinter Spring

for Greg, wherever he is

'Hard liquor', joints, and more than faded jeans:
The gestures of your otherness only show
You know this region better than you know;
Not what a landscape is but what it means.

You get it right: thus, 'unprepared and rested
Is better than unrested and prepared'.
Our friends were only ever those who dared
To put their friendship where it would be tested.

You give a steady trust, not easily
But where it most is needed or is earned.
You know how much of it will be returned,
More valuable than either dope or whisky

Or things that pass for love. And so, departing,
Seek out some limestone landscape after all,
Where people are themselves, and there recall
Mid-Anglia at this midwinter spring.

For You

A sudden solitude reveals itself
In ill-cooked meals, half-eaten; washing-up
Stacked jagged in the sink; bad sleep at night.
Or in a crowd I look around for you
As if you or your likeness could appear
Among the patchwork lights within the dark,
Among the minutes, silent and alone,
While the clock turns to a derelict November.

The grey has polarised to black and white,
The unreal clarity of an exploded view:
A local ailment blossoms to a blight –
The poverty of self-indulgence! True,
But those are all the words I'd have to write,
When all the other songs had failed, for you.

8 January 1974

Storms follow your departure: suddenly
I inhabit a community of rain.
A barn blown over, floods, a fallen tree
Map out the battered landscape. And again
Rain comes from each direction; every window
Crackles like static; the insistent blast
Rips honeysuckles from the wall as though
It means this January to be their last.

I lose myself in books as if the page
Could purge the weather of the memories
The storm has carried with it in its passage.
I think once more of other loyalties:
Letters to write, but nothing left to say.
The world had seemed much calmer yesterday.

Easter Sunday 1974

The shadow of the house lies on the lawn.
The vicar walks through sunlight on the road
To evensong. I puzzle in despair:
Should I, unchristian, find redemption there
Or must I look elsewhere for resurrection?
But he has disappeared: and here's the pen,
The paper for a statement – yes, my credit,
In love as in religion, overdrawn.

I know that I have overplayed my hand –
Reason enough for anyone to wonder
Which was the first, the quintessential blunder?
Outside, the light has dimmed insidiously;
The shadow of the house has climbed the trees.
I know that this is not the promised land.

24 April 1974

For you, I leave the other words unsaid,
Or say them to myself. It's getting near,
This end, too near to distance or to dread:
Activity kills time when time breeds fear.
If once I dreamed of effortlessly reaching
The fragrant plateau, then I was deluded;
My place is in the valley, learning, teaching,
And that is where my bargains are concluded.

'Anyway, thanks,' your letter ends. It's you,
My friend, to whom the deeper thanks are due,
And those who shared our crises, lost our sleep –
The friends we keep to have and have to keep.
We may no longer prosper and deceive
The other greater world. For you I leave.

6 May 1974

I pay this debt of friendship willingly.
You will and it is right you never know
How long those paragraphs were in my mind.
Remember how we spoke of empathy
In someone else's world, a life ago?
That region I shall never leave behind.
The here and now afflicts me like a cramp:
I seal the envelope; I lick the stamp.

Ellington is playing: yours and yours.
The years have coalesced without a pause:
I see their fabric not their pattern now;
That and the music's languid river flow
Towards eternity. You hear it. Thus,
You know too well what will remain of us.

Suffolk Poems

July, 1974

Summer blossoms in fuchsias,
geraniums, hollyhocks,
and pointless casual death.
The day before I arrived,
a local man was murdered:
'following an incident
outside an hotel,' a youth,
the paper tells me, was charged.

And within the same fierce week
visitors to the Tower
of London were killed or maimed
by an unwarned explosion.
I think, above all, of friends
trapped in embattled Cyprus,
hearing only their voices
in each day's six o'clock news.

It will get worse. This is not
hopeless fear or mere despair,
but the knowledge that we grow
into deeper local grief
or international sorrow.
So, thanks to the wild east coast,
its marshes, wheatfields, relics,
all these unlikely havens.

Crag Path

Do the gulls pose on flagpoles, breakwaters, applauding
            others' aerobatic gestures in mirthless
dull chuckles? Or, on the beach like birds of porcelain
            perched upon a tiled suburban mantelpiece,
do some train a proprietary eye on distance,
            less mobile than the shingle which supports them?
Here, colours usurped by the makers of paperware –
            pink, primrose, pale blue, indeterminate green –
decorate all the eccentric apparatus: steps,
            railings, shutters, balconies and verandas,
the crazy architecture where each inch of sea view
            is reason enough for structures which no child
would make in Meccano and hope to remain standing.
            Attics climb on tiled or turreted shoulders;
giddy towers rise straight-faced and lop-sided, and not one
            topples as it should into the grey North Sea.

At sunset, the couples arm in arm along Crag Path
        wander, pointing out the lifeboat, the folly,
that dear little cottage: exclamations of routine
        surprise, packaged delight, seeking no reply.
Their accents – Birmingham or Edinburgh or West Ham –
        give them away. What do they see or look for,
these Pevsners of prettiness, connoisseurs of quaintness?
        For the mere detail that makes this not like home?
On the Town Steps, a solitary cat surveys them,
        off-centre, just under halfway from the top;
I respect that asymmetrical contemplation.
        It glances downwards, tucks in its paws, and yawns.

Leiston Abbey

Ranulf de Glanville, Robert
de Ufford, your legacies
have weathered this rough climate
half-a-dozen centuries:
more potent, more angular
than you could imagine, your

second abbey stands among
the worshipping fields of grain,
as if the North Sea had flung
its whole weight upon the plain,
leaving these crags eroded
like relics on the sea bed.

A meeting of ages: near
the coast the power station
eyes the chapel at Minsmere
in silent confrontation
across the marshland which shields
sanctuary among wheatfields.

Iken

At Iken Cliff, the well-fed tourists gather;
caravans, ice-creams, parodies of pleasure

drifting irresistibly towards Cliff Reach
where moody children mope at the muddy beach;

and none thinks to seek for solitude downstream
where, framed by trees, St Botolph's church awaits them,

gaunt and roofless, unthatched by fire and by storm.
Decay has overtaken the postcard charm:

creepers in the tower challenge the bell-ropes;
a builder's sign recalls diminishing hopes

outside in the weed-choked churchyard. Iken lies
ruined at last after thirteen centuries,

echoes the collect for its founder: 'efface
we pray Thee the scars of our wounds and heal us'.

Orford

The eye with a single glance
takes in castle, church, and quay –
these emblems of endurance:
a complete community
where nothing was left to chance.

Some architect named progress
or random necessity
tamed the space from Orford Ness
to Tunstall, eternally
a fragment of Englishness.

Here is another world's end,
last haven in your journey:
trapped at a river's long bend,
eyed by castle, church, and quay –
this place the seasons defend.

Last Days

When seascape becomes familiar, when you know
at what time each ship will cross the horizon,
heading for which port, then it is time to go
back towards the land-locked plains of Huntingdon.

Some things defy all scrupulous inquiry,
belonging to someone else's past, giving
wrong directions, false hints, a desultory
nod and wink of secrecy. And soon, nearing

the last days of a long summer, you will scour
herbaceous borders for an opening bud
and find a drowsy bee on a late flower,
with November in your mind, frost in your blood.

Listen

Whether side-step or ascent
gets us there I hardly know:
the evening's intransigence
may be omen or portent;
objects may intrude, and no
carefully prepared defence

can protect us from them yet.
The river-mist will glisten
outside in the headlamps' gleam;
distances we must forget
are starred with cats' eyes. Listen:
the beetle nibbles the beam

and a million animals
perform their necessary
ceremonies around you
in the floorboards, ceilings, walls,
where each has his history.
Listen: how can we be true

to our world, to each other?
The nervous resolute mouse
behind the skirting is true
to hunger or cold weather
and the old warmth of a house.
Listen: the barn door swings to

and shrubs tap at the window
asking to let the world in.
To be encompassed by all
these lives and yet not to know
where to move, how to begin!
Listen: catch me as I fall.

An Autumn Letter to Roger Walton

The lesser poets are all writing letters
To imitate or emulate their betters –
All those bright observers and reviewers,
The smiling rats in verse's friendly sewers.
Yet, now that there are two in print from Mole,
It's time this fieldmouse tottered from his hole
To take a sniff at the autumnal air,
That chloroform for talent. To be fair,
Some years ago I dabbled in this medium,
Wrote an epistle of Wordsworthian tedium,
Dispatched it to Australia and found
I should have cultivated my home ground.

Perhaps at last the time has come to view
Some of the many yous who make up You.
The well-read kid enthusing in the garden
Over Baldwin, Beckett, or John Arden …
You'd brought from Suffolk a survival kit
That's served you well (and how you needed it):
How else endure a minor public school
Unless a rugby player or a fool?
And how surmount the claustrophobic code
Of desperate crammers in Old Brompton Road
Without the seedy and beguiling charms
Of beer and billiards in The Drayton Arms?
An artist's background? Yes, and what depresses
Is the decline of those schoolboy successes,
Which thankfully you weren't, the running-down
Of adolescent hero, saint, or clown;
None of these, your muddles got you though
The labyrinth of muddles all around you.

So you survive, and through what other scenes!
Parochial, with neither wish nor means

To disinherit my imagined spaces,
Worst audience for news of foreign places,
I found high summer tidings from the States
Hard to digest. Although the call dictates,
The quick response I found a shade unnerving:
Thus it's both ludicrous and reassuring
That you should land in Lewisham; a flat,
A Polish landlady, perhaps a cat
Or two …
                    Good place. At least you're out of range
Of witless concerts at the Corn Exchange,
At which unlikely Bethlehem is born
Tangerine Dream or Technicolor Yawn
(Of course, it's not the music that's so loud
But the lack of music). And the crowd
Has changed in Cambridge, or I'm over-wise:
A perfect autumn afternoon – clear skies,
Too clear, the buildings posed for photographs,
The trees for winter, and the air for laughs –
And all the faces either dull or sad,
No smile unstoned, no elegance unmad.
People talk too loud or not at all:
The bold advance foretells the vague withdrawal.

Such ancient mutterings! I dread to think
What sort of bore (if sanity and drink
Should grant longevity) I'll come to be.
You will forgive …
                          Remember late July,
In Cambridge, '72, outside The Mill,
Downing draught Guinness? When we'd had our fill,
We let the place engross us, both aware
Of sheer *duende*, sunlight, and fresh air.
That potent summer's sunlight in its beams
Held past and future, all the Cambridge dreams
And all the force that years of learning give –
The knowledge that the dead knew how to live.

That force is weakening. Fine scholars grow
Shrill, petulant, and powerless: they sow
Their barren seeds in unresponsive soil –
Minds melted into pleasure, not by toil
Honed into sharpness at the forge of time;
Minds which will never wrestle for a rhyme.

Preposterous digression – well, maybe:
But we agree on craft and clarity
And in your art as well as mine prefer
The well-wrought to the merely amateur.
The easy and the pleasurable betray
A mind to dullness and a world to clay:
The stoic path through grief or tragedy
Will win though may not see the victory.
Meanwhile I have a friend or two who'll earn
A place in any book of life, who'll turn
This bankrupt language to a dwelling-place
For form and clarity, the sense of grace.
If this devalued age deserves an art,
Or we deserve to give it one, let's start.

The Way Back

Amber streetlamps punctuate the night.
Their deviously analytic glare
Reveals a world created by the light:
Not what there is but what it shows is there.

A place without surroundings: linear edge
Usurps the processes of definition
From meadowland and forest, field and hedge.
Suburban night knows only this condition,

The emptied moon's apologetic husk
Outshone by haloed sodium overhead:
Always between, always this waking dusk.
Sleep, silence, darkness: absolutes are dead.

Beyond the outskirts to the motorway:
Dark claims its spaces, but the eye moves on
Towards another imitation day –
A town or roundabout on the horizon –

Until 'The North' proclaims a giant sign,
As if the north were somewhere you could reach
By following a disembodied line
Which joins nowhere to nowhere, each to each,

And work to home. Or will it merely end
In featureless space, an orange void stretching
On each side of the room, round the next bend,
With distant amber lamps, the planets, gleaming?

In a Cold Season

The resonant descant of a distant bird;
The water-butt's quick trickling percussion;
As an eye half-glimpses, there are things half-heard

Across a world vacated by the word,
In this still dusk, this breathless interruption.
The resonant descant of a distant bird

Quavering between perfect and absurd,
The utterance and the reverberation:
As an eye half-glimpses, there are things half-heard;

And each moves softly through the distance, blurred
As dusk descends upon a dream of reason.
The resonant descant of a distant bird

Hangs, brittle and resilient, undeterred
By clamouring showers in a cold season.
As an eye half-glimpses, there are things half-heard;

The dead and dancing leaves the breeze has stirred,
Mocking the silence, muttering of treason.
The resonant descant of a distant bird:
As an eye half-glimpses, there are things half-heard.

Chronology

John Dankworth's clarinet, recorded
the month I was born: disconcerted,

I fumble in the shelves, discover
he was twenty-one. Turning over

the record, there's *Mop Mop*: I've that, played
by the Hawk himself, half a decade

further back. Young John and Vic don't quite
get the tricky extra half-beat right:

forgive them for youth if it inspires
these hours among the Tempos, Esquires

Commodores, Savoys – so much to say
in each side. Old books can't talk that way.

A Spring Letter to Richard Monk

The bluebell season's over. Tattered petals
Survive among the bracken and the nettles,
Last remnants of a transitory spring
Much valued in its rapid vanishing.
The summer's brooding vigour lies in wait,
Like local thunder, claiming its estate
With armies of cow-parsley; sentries stand
On leafy guard in ceded meadowland.

Such unsurprising landscapes most surprise
By being richly there as legacies
Of other sparser seasons. Grand designs,
Mapped out by grid or megalithic lines,
Must take the details of regeneration
To be their starting-point and first foundation.
Look closer, for this latent land will yield
Worlds in a leaf, a universe in a field.

Yet at a point where those lines intersect
In May, you have a different prospect;
At least you'd think so. My guess in this game
Is that in fact the view looks much the same
From each end of the cosmic telescope:
As long as it's in focus then there's hope.
In Somerset, in Suffolk, landscapes bring
The ages' synthesis, true summit meeting.

The difference is only of degree:
Wordsworth at Tintern, you at Glastonbury
(Leaving Leiston Abbey out of this)
Are seekers after natural synthesis –
To 'see into the heart of things', an art
More arduous than seeing to the heart
Of nothing. Thus we need a clarity
Of vision, not the mind's blind chemistry.

Pedantic or paternal? (Both, you'd say,
Believing neither.) The brash getaway
Was ever just a cover-up for fear
In those who couldn't bear to stay and hear
Or wait and see: the lanes they travel through
Return, exhausted and indifferent, to
The neutral dust. Who cares for rabbits' rights
Within a world defined by wheels and lights?

All that's a shade allusive. Let's change gear
(My final – promise! – two-wheeled image here).
You'll say a hand-set, hand-sewn pamphlet's worth
Your bookshop full of Penguins: so the earth
Makes everything one-off. It's going fast,
For sure, and hard to tell if we're the last
Who'll strive to view things as they're meant to be,
Not for their use, but for their oddity.

The urge to breathe some uncorrupted air,
To take a more extended trip to where
Ideas have substance strong enough to keep;
The need for some imaginative leap –
Over the stile into the bluebell wood,
Or further, elsewhere, hardly understood –
Sustains. Before we're dead, we'd best be quick
But careful too. So watch the ripples, Dick.

At the Edge

Far inland this late July,
I imagine those coastlines –
Caernarvon, Sussex, Suffolk –
and think of you at the edge
of a well-studied ocean
whose dirty secrets emerge
numbered in tomato pips.

Through a vocabulary
which does what it has to do
with ungraceful exactness,
you express about the sea
things I shall never fathom,
confronting those mysteries
whose gift is their remoteness.

And yet, awed, intransigent,
I too must question; concoct
in the kitchen of ideas
the approximate flavour
of some finely-charted coast;
season it with the right words.
Scientist and writer are

not so different, perhaps …
Men who live on their edges,
inhabit borders, margins,
embody the coasts they crave
and need the answering clash
of waves over the shingle,
no metaphor but design.

1 August 1975

The buddleia's white-hot spears begin to rust;
A gasping sparrow staggers open-beaked
Across the flagstones; bumble bees get stuck
In sunny rooms; a year ago we met.

Time to revise love's lexicon again.
Shrub, sparrow, bee find their maturities.
Survivors struggle to the summer's brink
And celebrate in secret ceremonies.

A Late Summer Letter to Alec Chasemore

Five years have passed since first I tried this trick
To make the message of a letter stick:
And what began, for me, as a frail hope
Became a fashion, sanctified by Pope,
Performed by every virtuoso hack
Who, what's more, got published letters back.
So here's to you, John Fuller and Clive James,
James Fenton too, and other well-known names
Who've made a kind of rhyming Alan Brien
From an uncanny brew of skill and try-on
(That rhyme's at worst Clive Jamesian, so's this:
I write to take the biscuit, not the piss).
I like your poems and I wish you well:
To know so many people must be hell.

The preface done, the matter. Matthew's dead.
Full stops on either side leave much unsaid
Beyond the distant echo of a name.
We have a debt to settle and a claim

To make: for you and I, his closest friends,
Must recognise at last how friendship ends
Not in a word, a phrase, a scene, an act,
But in a random accidental fact.
Vulnerable, truthful, he could see
Abyss and summit simultaneously:
The friend who wouldn't fake it, whose despair
Engulfed like morning fog, cleared as the air
In autumn. Our experience is filtered,
As sunlight, and its radiance is altered;
But he admitted pure light's glare and heat,
Sought undiluted worlds and took them neat.
Who, sensing this, would grudge him his defence,
His eggshell-brittle cynical pretence?
What mocking grin would greet an elegy,
For Matthew was no Robert Gregory:
Poet, scholar, friend who saw us through
The best times and the worst, death's cheated you.

The argument's fragmented into splinters.
There's danger here: remember Yvor Winters'
Attack on Yeats and his attempts to muster
Legendary heroes from a cluster
Of friends and relatives and ancestors,
Great patriots, great artists or great bores.
Yeats had a thirst he plainly couldn't quench
(Do we really need to know of Mrs French?)
For true nonentities; and yet I feel,
Like Auden, 'Most at home with what is Real'.
Of course one should address the Fisherman
Who doesn't exist: I try to, but who can
Communicate for long with an idea?
Neither Yeats nor Auden could, that's clear
From all the real people in their pages
(Not to mention those gyrating sages).
The fact is that at times it's good to know
There's someone real out there, okay? Hello.

No doubt by now you've conquered Amsterdam
Accompanied by Simon, Neil and Ham –
Harmonious quartet, or maybe not
By now … in any case I'm sure you've got
What you want or need. (How's that intended?
Is it perhaps what's meant by open-ended?)
My travels of a more domestic sort
I should have finished; but it seems they're fraught
With every kind of legal complication
Which gives new meaning to the word 'completion'
That agents like so much. Thus incomplete,
I hardly dare to guess where next we'll meet
When you've returned to Wiltshire. Do the stations
And trains facilitate East-West relations?

There's autumn in the air, and there's the curse
Of English poetry: nostalgic verse
Brought on by modulations in the light,
The scent of bonfires, the descent of night.
And as the dead leaves gather in the gutter
So, on my desk, a sympathetic clutter
Will fall upon an overripe confusion
Or mask unfinished business with conclusion.
Our world grows smaller, Alec: dreams decay;
The rules are changed in games we used to play;
Our shrines are unremembered; our friends die.
To live, we have to learn to say goodbye.

A Cooling Universe

in memory of Matthew Desmond

1

The seasons rain on us continually,
Struck with the thunder of coincidence.
All we see of light is all we see,
Where darknesses admit no evidence
Except the final perjury of death.
Lineaments of autumn grid the page,
Flicker and jump like shadows on a hearth;
Thicken into furrows; lose their edge,
Distorting as a cloud crosses the sun,
A bird the sky, a branch the window-pane.
Conclusions signal something new begun
And histories convoked. Thus we remain
  While swallows in their purposeful migrations
  Enact the comedy of generations.

2

Enact the comedy of generations
Or else rewrite the plot; but what director
Would countenance the follies and frustrations,
The miscued lines, steps out of character
Of one predestined actor cast to choose?
Upon a littered desk the objects wait
Which have no business here but to confuse
With empty myths: old shrines we consecrate
At random visits – papers, notes and letters.
Is this the past? Redundancies of love,
Relinquished loyalties, discarded fetters:
Props too entrenched and seasoned to remove,
  Assembled as a botched-up tragedy.
  We turn their progress into history.

3

We turn their progress into history
Reversed out in a fading retrospect
By modulations to a minor key
Whose flattened thirds diminish the prospect.
Themes mingle in a child's kaleidoscope,
Distant and inexplicable, beyond reach,
In whose waking abandonment grows hope.
Music and colour surface on a beach,
Fused to a single sense: this is the way
It is when outside history and time
We see ourselves. The play becomes replay.
All sound resolves into a single chime:
      In clinging echoes, lingering vibrations,
      The air reveals its ghostly intimations.

4

The air reveals its ghostly intimations
Between last blossom and first blighted leaf:
A hinterland upon the map of seasons,
The neutral zone dividing death from grief.
Swift evening chills the amber afternoon
As, in the angles of refracted light,
The legend crystallises all too soon,
Set in relief against oncoming night.
Now in the gathering dusk where dreams begin,
The picture jigsawn into jagged parts,
We seek a frame to fit the pieces in
Or way to navigate the tangled charts:
      New islands in the mind, new continents
      Emerging in their late embodiments.

5

Emerging in their late embodiments,
The random days reconstitute a past:
We forge such fragments into monuments,
From ruins fabricate a world to last,
Composed of all the small eternities:
The breathless evenings when the mist closed in
Or embers flared in brief epiphanies
Absolving countless centuries of pain.
And thus it is the long perspective alters,
Losing itself in what envisaged it:
Facts clarify, imagination falters;
All that had seemed contained is infinite.
       Our myths will nourish us from year to year:
       They luminously glow, then disappear.

6

They luminously glow, then disappear:
It is the glancing after-light sustains
Through fractured love and superstitious fear
And what remains after the waste remains.
By charting time we find the timeless space:
The church behind the pig-sty compassing
Its infinite locality of place
Where being flowers out of visiting;
Secrets of a rainy summer wait,
Encoded, for the key which would reveal
Much to forgive and all to mitigate,
The self-inflicted wounds which will not heal.
       We come through time as suffering penitents
       Into the order of the elements.

7

Into the order of the elements,
The palsied purities of fire and ice,
We drift: impelled by endless tides and currents
Which rise as whirlpools and will not suffice
Unless to guide us to oblivion.
Death is the mother of nothing but desire
For time and energy to carry on
Against the furnace or the glacier.
A partial light illuminates these days,
Enduring although flecked with driving rains,
Chequered with leafless branches, and always
Fading: yet what thou lovest well remains.
       Dates indicate the fag-end of the year;
       At the poem's centre, meanings become clear.

8

At the poem's centre, meanings become clear:
Now (almost settled in my house) I find
The soul, still guest and not possessor here,
Hankering after something left behind.
Old tenants of this masonry persist –
Pale translucent moths which cling to beams,
Motionless for days and frail as mist,
Inhabitants of ruins or of dreams;
A single clumsy wasp; and in the grass
A resolute, self-confident bullfinch
Who seems to think that I, like time, will pass.
I claim my territory inch by inch,
       My implement a hand-trowel not a spade,
       The pattern of a world to be remade.

9

The pattern of a world to be remade
Upon the map, the same geography,
The board on which the other games were played,
Their spaces planed to domesticity:
Perhaps the mocking bullfinch understands
How scales must coexist – the sky, the nest;
How details spring from unremembered lands
Spread out below in flight – a palimpsest
Anonymous yet pregnant with the traces
Of previous encounters; homing, how
Our landmarks are the half-forgotten places
Where then entangles with the here and now;
      How, on returning, we at best may reap
      The harvest of a habitat to keep.

10

The harvest of a habitat to keep:
A safe stronghold! Such insularity!
A castle or a hole in which to creep,
Great enterprise or eccentricity?
'The writer as linguistic polymath':
Finding in Steiner this impressive phrase,
I ponder: having sought the narrow path,
Its picturesque diversions through the maze
Of learning. Gaudy plants burst into flower,
Competing in their brash proliferation:
Not Ballylee but Babel is the tower
Where blooms may thrive upon deracination.
      In avenues at evening, in the shade,
      Our legends live as they begin to fade.

11

Our legends live as they begin to fade:
Only a journal's neatly dated pages
Preserve notations, evidence displayed
To time, whose cool indifference assuages
So much that seemed in vain or hard to tell
Or merely ludicrous. This parasite
Of a blotchy past – all anecdote and libel,
Indulgences of whisky and midnight –
Still clings: a history of trivia;
A survey of decisions undecided;
An inventory of impedimenta,
Life's modest clutter, easily derided;
      And griefs for which it is too late to weep
      As time and distance beckon us to sleep.

12

As time and distance beckon us to sleep,
Lines soften into shadows. Here at least
Bleak landscape and clear light may help to keep
A style plain as the wheatfields of the East
Or other regions whose topography
Enforces its unwritten discipline –
Llano and tundra, wilderness and scree,
Where space and sparseness suddenly align.
Such landscapes should dictate a clarity
Of vision, an economy of words,
A still life rather than a tapestry:
We see the trees because there are no woods.
      Lines soften: thus for landscape and for verse
      The curtain falls on all we could rehearse.

13

The curtain falls on all we could rehearse.
The opening chords of winter's overture
Sound in the distance like a muttered curse
From ancient giant ghosts, the last of laughter.
Once the grave was merely metaphor,
Death a necessity acquitted by
Infirmity or age, where to have gone before
Proclaimed departure: the obituary
Of ancestors is written by our lives;
The autumn of the body is a season
Witnessed by every child in relatives.
Mortality evolves from myth to reason.
       The past a loan we cannot reimburse,
       Hot fragments of a cooling universe.

14

Hot fragments of a cooling universe
Survive among the glacial confusion;
A first death met on equal terms is worse
Than every other well-prepared conclusion.
Time dusts an empty stage where silver light
Lets details and delineation fade,
Sharp contrasts and reflections melt from sight.
The images of summer have decayed
Like overripened and unharvested
Blackberries rotting in an unknown lane,
Waiting for extinction's sombre tread.
Stark branches and a falling sky remain;
       The swallows and the shadows leave the tree;
       The seasons rain on us continually.

15

The seasons rain on us, continually
Enact the comedy of generations;
We turn their progress into history.
The air reveals its ghostly intimations
Emerging from their late embodiments;
They luminously glow, then disappear
Into the order of the elements
At the poem's centre. Meanings become clear:
The pattern of a world to be remade,
The harvest of a habitat to keep.
Our legends live: as they begin to fade,
As time and darkness beckon us to sleep,
      The curtain falls on all we could rehearse,
      Hot fragments of a cooling universe.

II
1976–1986

Teasels

Teasels lean their enquiring stems
Towards me across the shadowed room.
The one on the right is listening.

They stand in a solid Cotswold pot
As if for a launching. They ought to go off
At mad angles, like demented rockets.

Such bristling energy in death!
They seem more alive than the plants
Which weep for water or for warmth.

Theirs is a last bleak independence,
Scorning nourishment and care,
Unwilling to entertain a duster.

The Black Bechstein

G.A.T., 1964

I was late on the scene.
Some timbers still smouldered,
Though most were dust by then
As, like the conclusion
Of a Victorian disaster
In industrial engineering,
The piano's skeleton uttered
Its final fractured notes
From random, cooling strings.

I was an adolescent,
Moved more by the occasion
Than what it meant. And yet,
A foolish schoolmaster,
Fellow-musician and thus
Not your favourite colleague
(All staffrooms are like that)
Thought I, your pupil, might best
Tell you the worst.

I found you in the garden.
I chatted casually.
You'd taught me this, for you'd
Begin each lesson that way,
Lowering the tension
Before a note was played.
I told you in your own
Calm tone: the music rooms;
Your Bechstein; all
Destroyed.
                You thanked me,
Went on digging quietly.

No other place or piano
Would do. You never forgave
The bringer of bad news,
And I could never forgive
Myself that self-importance,
The awful sense of occasion.
I'd be a pianist, if ...

But there it was: we quarrelled –
Your lonely resentment
And my arrogant defences –
Until I walked out, leaving
You to contemplate
The callousness of children.

Early Summer

Upsetting the long-stay neurotic sparrows,
New patients check in: ballooning wood-pigeons,
Indignant at my trespass in their province,
Scrabbling off the ground when caught in a corner,
Embarrassed at getting airborne;
                                        then their foils,
Wheeling and screaming in the walled garden, swifts,
Clinging to invisible banked circuits of sky,
Scything the overgrown afternoon;
                                        the summer
Framed by extremes of elegance and speed.

Four Quarters

North

Some people and the north wind seem to wait
Round blind corners for surprised encounters.

Sunlight fractures in the brittle air,
Dazzles from redundant puddles, windows,

And in odd angles of contorted trees.
Iron twigs litter the ground; milk-bottle tops

Scuttle along the street; the morning breathes
An amazed gasp of adversity, of life.

East

Snow grits the earth like dusty splinterings
Of a distant frozen planet breaking up.

Some granulated arctic mineral,
Sprinkled from a cosmic pepper pot,

Garnishes with winter's condiment
The nervous spring's uncertain vegetation.

Sheer pretence! The pavement reasserts
Its wet grey mastery at every step.

South

Insomnia on a sweaty April night:
Shades of sirocco in North Hertfordshire.

Wizened old stems of an hibiscus sprout
Anaemic and unprecedented shoots

As if put out, as I am, by the warmth
Of a transparent suffocating blanket

Gently settling on the universe,
Breezing away the dominion of air.

West

The west wind stiffens as the rain comes on.
The church tower vanishes into stone sky.

Blossoms enact unseasonable autumn,
Flutter across a screen of monochrome.

The sound of distant traffic conjures up
Wet homeward journeys on forgotten roads.

Past and present dance outside the window,
Rejoicing in the end of a dry season.

The Bridge

One stands above an upstream cutwater,
Rod angled aimlessly towards the land,
Safe in his niche; while on the other side
His friend leans on the opposite pilaster,
Arms braced against the stone and legs astride
As if to clasp the bridge with either hand.

There are no fish. The first knows this and smiles:
It is enough to be a part of air
And sun and stone and water, bridging them.
His line into the river runs for miles,
Transfigured from the rod's initial stem
Into the web of currents everywhere.

His friend feels none of that. He stares downstream
Where sunlight catches an abandoned tyre
And glances back in glossy insolence,
Hardened into a rigid silver gleam.
The clasp upon the parapet grows more tense.
Sweat chills his neck. The stonework is on fire.

Between the bridge's piers the river brings
Its casual luggage and its fluent art
Past those whom it will neither curse nor bless:
One is detached because a part of things,
The other restless in his separateness.
The bridge which bears them carries them apart.

The Other Night

I dreamt of you the other night. It seems
The fractured days reticulate my dreams.

First there were the retrospects, the glances
At real events and places, hopes and chances,

From which I woke to the anaemic glow
Outside the clarifying dawn window,

Pretending 'I knew it couldn't be' – and still
In time I learnt to dream that codicil.

So, the other night, I must have cried,
'It can't be – it's a dream'; but you replied,

'It's not, it's real: the other was the dream.'
Convinced, I tried to comprehend the scheme,

Only to wake: the same walls, the same ceiling.
Soon I shall learn to dream the reawakening.

Does this mean I shall wake among the dead?
Memories unwind inside my head.

Somewhere

Logs are being sawn somewhere:
Easing through the softened air,

Heavy with rain and sodden leaves,
The sound of blade on timber gives

An edge to cloud's infinities.
Mist buttresses the nervous trees,

Smoke jostles where the cloud persists,
But there below the saw persists.

The blade gives edge to what it takes.
The world is split. The timber breaks.

Sur la Terrasse

a painting by David Hockney

Limits: distance and near edge.
Here you are contained, and yet
hills and trees delineate
a further world. The curtains
know their place and hesitate,
held back, restrained: open doors
are the best we can hope for.

But listen. Don't turn. There is
another distance within
where the eye shapes, translating
image into imagery:

beyond the curtains, casting
a separate glance and now
a shadow within shadow.

Being and seeing are more
than the best we could hope for:
now all the generous light
is yours. On the terrace you
keep distance and edge in sight
and are them, contained: see how
the shadows bend towards you.

The Vanished Places

At Dunwich, you feel like a trespasser on the earth:
        on sunken paths through the mushroom-scented wood
past the last monastery wall and the last gravestone
        (John Brinkley Easey, uneasy at the brink)
to the cliffs' edge and the last church tower out at sea.
        They say the bells still peal, perhaps to restore
some tenuous hope of immortality, while bones
        gesture a final desultory farewell.

Trespasser? Tenant? Neither will win, the sea insists,
        in the vanished places – Dunwich, Walberswick –
where lanes scrawl to the margin of a torn-off coastline
        whose history is rewritten by the tide.
Think, the sea persists, of your monuments and cities,
        skills and crafts, in the scale of natural time;
and then remember eleven Dunwich churches drowned
        off this temporary coast; tread carefully.

Too simple to wish a lingering death concluded:
     'the halo of traditionary splendour'
(the Reverend Alfred Suckling, 1848)
       still glimmers here in the wasted vacancy.
A scything north-easterly wind, sleet across the sea,
      and a burdened sky weigh down upon the land:
trespasser, tenant, walk tentatively here,
     your world undercut by erosive waters.

A Season of Calm Weather

1. *A Mossy Wall in Sidgwick Avenue*

Random, the resurfacing of pain:
A mossy wall in Sidgwick Avenue
And, on the path, familiar slur of leaves …

Why should this bite? Why should it, come to that,
Conjure a false familiarity
In one by choice unCantabrigian?

Such pangs are symptoms of uncharted loss,
Snapshots of another, fictive life
Brought quickly into focus, brightly lit.

Resurfacing of pain: bringing to light.
Yet, not to evade a small semantic tangle,
Resurfacing a path is covering up.

To cover up the pain I kick the leaves
Which covered up the path, resurfacing
A little of the random world, like rain.

2. Beyond My Means

I gather that I live beyond my means.
'DR,' the statement stutters: short for 'drat',
I'd like to think, or maybe even 'drunk'.

No such luck: the message, clear enough,
Is more diluted special-offer scotch,
The twelve-year-old malt banished to the past.

Outside, the mortgaged world is freezing hard,
And I at last ironically a 'member'
Of a Building Society! Will it help or matter

That this one has a poet on its board?
By all accounts, our poems will be worth
As little as our love, less than our shares.

Obscure, unquoted, my duodecimo portion
Of a Chaplinesque Bolivian tin mine
May yet surprise us all, an old friend says.

Early for the weather forecast, I hear
The FT Index closed at 409.
Good news, it seems. Means may catch up with me.

3. Aftermath

'I heard the Stones at Madison Square,' you said,
Shyly. I liked that. After all the fuss
The others made at Knebworth for the Floyd,

For 'festivals' on bogged-down, windswept fields,
Reluctant understatement stopped them dead.
Where did you learn to try not to impress?

4. *North Hertfordshire*

Pesthouse Lane, Dead Street, and Limekiln Lane
Are Clothall Road, Queen Street, and Kingsland Way:
The Ministry of Truth's at work again.

Strange, this desire to cover up the past,
Its plain style of abrasive honesty,
As if the past might give too much away.

In Pepper Alley, off the Market Place
(The name no doubt retained through oversight),
Spices were sold; here cautious windows peep

With sidelong glances down high walls inscribed
'Lincoln Boot Boys', 'Blacks Out', 'Spurs OK'.
What's happened to the language of the tribe?

5. *At Baldock*

Silas Howes, Swan Brand, and Plummer Craft,
Their names and times Dickensian, reproach
Incurious passers-by, late daffodils.

Emboldened letters, weather-eaten words
Outstare a hundred years to tell us all
Their widows thought that we should know of them.

'Wife of the above': things said, unsaid.
A century of winters keeps intact
Relationships, degrees, each in his place.

'Thomas Rodd, of London.' Far away:
A place to be of, come from, ending here
Beneath brave stones in foreign Hertfordshire.

6. *A Sleevenote on the Goldberg Variations*

To earn a footnote in some history;
To slide through time, like Goldberg, by mistake;
To gain a niggling notoriety …

These are the gentler and the nobler fames,
Distinguished by their pure contingency,
Their guileless innocence of clever games

And ways to make a splash. We cannot choose
The resonances which attach to names,
Nor can we, thus immortalised, refuse

To designate a rose or dead-end street;
A set of variations or a blues;
A plain stone or an ornamental seat

Inscribed 'In memory of' beside a lake;
A square, a hall, a place where people meet
And take our names in earnest, by mistake.

7. *The Future*

I walk through the silent town. A breeze is blowing
Snuffed-out candles from horse-chestnut trees.
The unknown is on the air, and I am knowing

Something I cannot recognise, unless
It is a distant prospect of the future, showing
All that is and all that will come to be,

As blossoms of the past are going, going.

Return Trip

Caught in a gauze of sunlight,
you form into the image
of previous encounters:
it's strange how the eye transfers
each nuance, however slight,
from your other former age.

And the distance between us!
Knowing each other's neglect,
fearing each other's reproach,
the matters we dare not broach
must for a while elude us;
for what else should we expect

in the gentle thaw after
a winter so long ago?
Could in a trap that sunlight
springs to contain them, the right
words come gradually, and here
they are. Welcome back. Hello.

The Last Field

In the last field he would pause before the stile,
Look back across the furrowed ploughland, know
The lineaments of landscape as his own:
Time-softened hillsides; fences overgrown;
The muddy lower field; the lusher meadow;
A dog-legged footpath limping mile on mile.

And always, here, an image: one weekend,
Home from school for half-term in November,
He had surveyed this huddled group – the spire,
The farmhouse and the ragstone barns – and higher,
Held in the charcoal sky, a single ember,
The swollen smouldering sun, poised to descend.

He watched until the barns eclipsed them, then
Stood motionless in gathered dusk and mist:
Land taking texture from the ragstone walls,
Hardening, darkening in the slow withdrawals
Of colour, light, and clarity. At last,
He turned towards his homeward path again.

He crossed the stile and wandered on, his task
To draw his mind from the encroaching land.
The image lingered as it lingers still:
Thus, following the dog's-leg path downhill,
I scan the ragged skyline as I stand
Before the stile, forging a homeward mask.

Old School Tie

Crumpled at the back of the bottom drawer:
Sevenoaks School Lists, 1964.
And here they are, lined up, like guests invited
To a formal function, and my name included
Among the strangers. I can't put a face
To any of them. 'Hardly knew the place,'
I try to kid myself in disbelief:
But seven years, a quarter of my life,
Must have left some residue …
                                        And yes,
Something is shaping from the emptiness:
Detached but clear, an accent or a voice,
A sharp eye's glance, a wry smile, a grimace.
In detail, though I cannot see them whole,
These faces are familiar after all.
Now, as the looks and gestures come together,
I find the strangers find they know each other,
Like people at a party who discover
After the second drink they've shared a lover
Or eaten at a restaurant in Rome
That only they have heard of. They're at home
In each other's company, but where am I?
Or rather, where was I?
                                    The diary:
First Assembly; First Form Order; First
XV v. Eltham, no doubt watched and cursed;
Thursday Club Elections; YFC
Meeting and Film; Choral Society;
U. 13 v. King's School, Rochester …
Predictable: but Visitation of Master,
Pipemakers' Company, is put in place
By HALF TERM after it, in uppercase,
An honour shared with SCHOOL PLAY and DISMISSAL,
But not with Chapel, Day Boys' Medical,

Masters' Meeting, Corporate Communion,
Nor even, sadly, with O.S. Reunion –
An event I'd never thought about till now,
Though in a way this is one.
                              I wonder how
They recognise each other. Badged and labelled?
Ranged by degree, high tabled and low tabled?
And do they talk of mortgages and shares,
Wives, children, gardens, jobs, commuter fares?
Or with some wild unbottled urgency
Boozily confess: 'I faked the try
Which won the Junior League in '62';
'I fancied you when you were twelve'; 'I drew
That sketch of Ernie?' No, the ghosts agree.
Cook, Jenkins, Tibbitts, Hornsby, Somner, Snee:
What did become of them? And what of me?

Days

Some days promise well. Refracted sun,
Cut by others' glass, enlightens mine;
The curtains warm where, luminous as wine,
Light seeps between the ended and begun;
At last the shapes of midnight disarray
Are redrawn in the brittle lines of day.

Already clouds obstruct the common light:
The gleam has gone – we missed it once again
And now the world seems, as it is, mundane.
Orange juice, toast, coffee, the quick bite
For breakfast and the newspaper's quick read:
Each satisfies a habit, not a need.

And the edenic dawn? No more than rest
Doing its job, easing us through its phase
Of waking optimism. What are days
But different ways of failing, or at best
Of seeming to succeed? How well we seem,
Depending on the state of mind or dream,

Will not in fact reveal how well we are.
The morning folds; the afternoon spreads out
Its greying manifesto; care and doubt
Thicken in the unconditioned air.
Slowed and dyspeptic after lunch we find
Surrounding us the dull lethargic grind

Which trades as working, earning, getting on.
Words fall like slabs to pave our arguments
While elsewhere, naggingly, the mind presents
An image of … it could be anyone,
Through all the sad delusions, all the pain,
Going downhill, alone, into the rain.

Sunday

Green upon green, the summer closes in
On banks and hedges where leaf fingers leaf.
We walk the fields after a night of rain,
Catch on the breeze land's heavy-breathed relief
That, after all, the green has come again.

The path forks here: a gate, a well-kept wood,
And yet the common greenness binds me still –
As if the grasses' sap were in my blood –
To this straight track which beckons us uphill
Towards some little summit of the world.

Sunday consigns last night to history.
The light rebukes the dark's indulgences:
All the lost hours of music, smoke and whisky
And half-truths stumbling on their own defences
Disperse into the overwhelming sky.

Up here, only the dancing skylarks stay
With us until at last we turn again
Towards the mapped-out land, spread in display.
On a line which joins your town to mine, a train
Is burrowing into the hillside, far away.

Toadflax

'Never,' says Grigson, 'be seduced by toadflax.'
He means of course *Linaria Vulgaris*,
The yellow stuff which 'spreads incessantly':
Each 'quarter-inch of root breeds a new plant'.

Perhaps he'd look more kindly on the spikes
Of *Linaria Purpurea* in rubbled corners,
Clinging to the interstices of walls,
Bravely tenacious, however downtrodden.

Not for the first time, I find myself wishing
That plants could give us some tips on survival.
My anthropomorphic vote goes to Toadflax:
Good name for a rabbit in *Watership Down*.

Out of Time

I come to you again
Across the years; across
The miles of poppies, gorse,
And tattered villages;
Across the line between
The Midlands and the East
Where land gives way to sky;
Across the Suffolk plain.

Walking along the shore
Beneath the mallowed wall
To the Martello tower,
Knowing these limits now,
These shifting constancies
Of tides and boundaries,
At last I learn the pace
I should have learnt before.

My prison is the sea:
You rule my movements now
And make me move with you.
I come here willingly
Yet when I go, I go
Against my will and yours.
You liberate, enclose:
My prison sets me free.

I hear this song once more
After a dozen years:
Unnerving synthesis
Of timelessness and time.
Chris Farlowe sings it still
On a juke-box in the pub –
Summer of '66,
The future all in store –

Time-capsule of a song!
This continuity
Of shingle and of sea,
Past-self and future-self,
As faded summers flare
In a song across a bar,
Reminds me that I've 'been
Away for much too long'.

A dozen years have passed
Since I paced out this shore,
Full of unripened plans
Of all there was to be done:
Of all I could have done
In a dozen empty years!
I should have stayed at first.
I shall remain at last.

Windows

First and best is a window to the sea
When homing fishing-boats are silhouettes
As early sunlight tints the empty beach;
Or when, past shadowed shingle, water glows
In slow dusk and the flecking lighthouse-beam
With triple gesture comforts, charms and warns.

The second window opens onto plains
Where wheatfields stretch from nearby ear and stem
Until the stared-at skyline disappears.
In winter, stripped, the earth reveals itself:
Its muscular and bleak topography
Teaches endurance, promises rebirth.

Third and last is a window onto trees.
It will do for now: I like this filtered light.
The willow dusts the grass; the copper beech
Has weathered its long autumn gracefully;
And soon, when leafless branches web the sky,
The trees will show new lines, lucidities.

Stages

for Ben Staines and Tim Watson

1. *The Prologue*

He's part of the scene. He gestures
Disdainfully towards action,
Outlines a map on which honour
And dishonour form the contours.

He's above such paltry matters
As treachery, loyalty, love:
The deaths of fools and princes
Are ancient history to him.

He apologises slyly
For his world's deficiencies:
You will kindly imagine
An army, a fight now and then.

He's on your side really:
He hopes you won't heckle
Or insist on a refund,
Yet he doesn't trust actors.

He won't go away. He belongs.
At home you'll discover him
Washing up, gardening,
Cooking: part of the scene.

2. *The Tent*

Again they call. They pester, and I grow
Hour by hour more obdurate – 'obtuse'
The prissy politicians say – although
Ulysses must know why I refuse
His eloquent requests. Not vanity
But strength with which he justly credits me
Insists that I pursue the life I choose
And counteracts his cool diplomacy.

They use more language than they understand:
Their schoolboy honour is a travesty
To make a childish scrap in no-man's land
Into a battle fought for king and country.
This silly prank is Menelaus' game –
His bitchy wife, his folly, and his shame.
Chucking him was sense, not destiny:
If I'd been Helen, I'd have done the same.

And yet we came and did our best to please,
Playing by their rules. 'Splendid,' they said.
'Don't stop: your reputation tarnishes
Unless you keep it polished till you're dead.'
Their honour comes with that persuasive catch,
A built-in bribe to keep you up to scratch:
One false move, and honour's disappeared,
For who recalls the star of last year's match?

But life and sport are really not the same
(They'd find the difference inconvenient).
When I'm a corpse I'll have no taste for fame;
Till then, my taste demands life's nourishment:
Food, drink, and love are all that's precious.
Again they call. What will become of us?
They speculate and sneer at our intent.
Let Agamemnon stew. More wine, Patroclus.

3. *A Death*

The day recedes. Blood floods across the plain.
There suddenly is nothing left to say,
Nothing to do but turn around again.
You should have known that it would end this way.

Now what you could not do is done at last –
'Achilles hath the mighty Hector slain' –
And what you could not be is in the dust
Behind your horse. Your triumph is in vain.

A hero for a corpse is poor exchange
On either side, and this especially,
Of all beautiful losers. And that's strange:
For he now is where you feel you should be,

As legend crystallises from his past.
You watch the clinging failure of your schemes:
You drove a bargain too hard and too fast,
And sheltered kids grow up to have bad dreams.

4. *A Dream*

In a dream I wake within the empty space:
There must be someone in this cold dark place.

In a dream the lights are out, the doors are locked,
The entrances and exits are all blocked.

In a dream the flats collapse, the rostra split:
Battlements litter the abandoned set.

But when did everybody disappear?
Why did the actors go and leave me here?

In a dream at last I reach the bedside light
Which makes dreams worse: which makes them infinite.

5. *Give Me Some Light*

I think I begin to get the hang of this:
'Cue thirty it is, according to my text.
Do we agree? Yes, I want everything,
The whole damn lot. It's *meant* to dazzle them.'

At 2 a.m. there'll be the three of us,
Learning the hard-won intimacy which comes
From working through our breaking points. 'I've spent
Sixteen hours on this fucking set today.'

So's he, and he. It's a complicity
We share, this special energy we know
Is given only for a certain time
To recreate a truth: the play's the thing.

Or so for the time being we'll pretend.
A week from now we'll be ourselves again,
But when tomorrow night the king cries out
'Give me some light!' we'll give him all we've got.

6. *Soliloquy*

I listen to you speak, hear only tone;
I feel the weight of words, not what they mean.
And this seems strange, in words so used and known,
But is (I know not *seems*) not strange at all.
For words are shadows which we move between
From light to light where heavily they fall.
You do not speak thus when we are alone.

I watch you ageing, see you only young.
The world, unweeded, grows from flower to seed,
To ripe and rot; yet here upon the stage
The time is broken, out of joint indeed:
For years are prisms which we move among,
Casting their fractured light from age to age …
'But break my heart, for I must hold my tongue.'

7. *Woe or Wonder*

It's our last night. Out front, I think of you,
Your calm hand restless on the cue-light switch,
Remembering our first night: a circuit blew
And left you guessing, cueless, in the dark.

The lightning storms among the battlements,
Flickers across the auditorium.
Backstage, beyond the wild and whirling words,
You make things work. The players come and go

Where we have placed them, more or less, and so
The evening gathers its contained momentum.
I watch, you hear: we're both spectators now
As this frail wooden O spins on until …

The rest is silence. Darkness will descend,
And all for this? 'What is it you would see?
If aught of woe or wonder, cease your search':
For what we judge, are judged by, is the end.

Solstice

December sun takes aim across the trees;
        Time pauses here;
Light finds among the boughs' interstices
        A rested year.

'So hallowed and so gracious is the time …'
        The shadows run
Along the winter's stage in silent mime:
        Things lost, begun.

With the Sea

And all of us seek transactions with the sea.
Permanently shifting, it is the permanent force
    in our shifting lives; so we edge to the coast,
the quiet stony beach, the silted estuary,
    knowing what to expect and finding surprise,
a new light reflected across familiar water.
    And thus our returns, if not always happy,
are at any rate truthful: bright redefinitions
    of our place in life, with the sea insisting
on its right as the source of our selves and our emblems.
    The dogs bringing driftwood, patient retrievers,
seem to hint at some need in the human condition;
    kids skimming pebbles, encamped night fishermen
are celebrants too of a secret communion;
    bather and sailor, artist and craftsman share
epiphanies: as through the sea-mist, discovered sun
    lights upon the suddenly envisioned waves.

Off the Map

1

It's here, at last, I feel
the space, the sense of air
at this bleak intersection:

a Victorian Tolly pub,
a garage opposite,
lost among fields and sky.

I'd imagine stopping here
at the dusk of an ancient day,
choosing among the roads,

asking, like Cobbett, my way
of labourers over their ale,
but knowing each way's away

from here, where all ends.
It's strange how the mind clears
out here, with nothing to view

but the good earth, the near sky,
the air falling over the wheat:
the best and the worst it can do.

2

Here I slow down, between
two known points: to the north,
the power station hums;

to the south, a cardboard resort,
its weatherboarded charm
and its bathers are out of sight.

A mile or so, no more,
yet it's nearly peaceful here
beneath the still crumbling cliff:

peaceful enough for the mind
to change gear for a while,
to dwell on the shifting shore.

For a while: a predatory car
perches on top of the cliff
and its occupants spill out,

deck-chaired and radioed, taking
their pleasure. Pleasure! May
heaven protect me from that.

3

I must try for a line
like the line of landscape,
taut, East Anglian;

like this bridleway,
stretched between meadows,
hung out to dry.

'Delineate', 'linear'
are charmed derivatives
for poet, cartographer:

a grid of textures,
both method and limit,
through which to disclose

stances, predicaments,
juxtapositions,
and realignments.

Hawker at Morwenstow

for Steve Goard

East Anglia, North Cornwall … peninsulaic:
Regions which lead to nowhere but the sea.
And he was drawn to water more than most:
To Morwenstow, by birth, by destiny,
A craggy battlefield for soul and ship,
And every wreck's embodiment a ghost.

Caught between sense and spirit! What he saw
Buckles his words and surfaces instead
In beached emblems: the *Caledonia*'s
White figurehead, 'the relique of the storm',
Over her captain's grave; above the cliff,
Hawker's hut, trained on the waves and weathers.

'Again startled! "A woman Sir, has brought
A man's right foot"'; 'A mangled seaman's heart';
'In every gust … a dying sailor's cry';
Charted by disaster, the years passed,
Chequered with faces like the *Alonzo*'s crew –
Their 'expression of reluctant agony'.

Unburied names: *Phoenix, Caledonia,*
Margaret Quayle, Alonzo, Avonmore …
'God is angry with this land,' he said,
'And so I think and fear.' His fears became
Both mask and habit, fracturing with time,
Flaking beneath 'the weather of suicide'.

No doubt he was mad at last, 'so racked and strained'
By ceaseless defeated labour. Then came ghosts.
'They thrill like an echo,' he wrote of them; 'no sound
But the words are felt all through.' Voice of the sea,
And pledge of Hawker's immortality:
'I would not be forgotten in this land.'

Crabbe at Aldeburgh

The saltmaster's son returned. Half-qualified,
Half-dreamer, half in love, and out of luck.
'Mask-*ill* – Mask-*ill*; and so you shall find me,'
Roared his employer when called by Crabbe 'Maskwell'.
But the new young 'doctor' found small employment,
His head full of botany, poetry, Miss Elmy.

Yet he remained, drawn to the protestant coast,
The poor quay at Slaughden, the splintered buildings.
1st of January 1779:
'Eleven houses were at once demolished …
He saw the breakers dash over the roofs,
Curl around the walls … crush all to ruin.'

1780, London: 'the miserable year,'
Says the biographer son, 'that he spent in the City …
Nothing but disappointments and repulses.'
Crabbe's Journal, though, is brightly alert,
His patience rewarded by Burke's benevolence –
One hundred pounds – and then by Holy Orders.

So the saltmaster's son returned to the mean town,
'A man of acknowledged talents; a successful
Author … and a clergyman.' His feelings 'may
Easily be imagined'; and so may his welcome.
'Unkindly received … I had too much indignation
To care,' he admitted, 'what they thought of me.'

Embittered, he stayed only months as curate; thence,
To uneasy luxury as Chaplain at Belvoir.
It is the poems which betray him in their clear
Sight and sound of a coast you cannot leave,
The abrasive edge of solitude, for 'there
A sadness mixes with all I see or hear'.

Iken, Again

Things were: a thriving river port …
Jumbo's Cottage, once the Anchor Inn,
Above the reach; St Botolph's island church,
Now roofless, land-linked and more desolate;
All but the flagrant gorse dissolved in grey.

Things were: a place to stir the Grimes in us,
Glimpsing the past by mudflats at low tide
In whitened skeletons of salted trees.
We grow into echoes. This too is
A place where prayer has been valid.

The Noble Truce

You are elsewhere. I wander
through space your absence creates:
the punctual hibiscus
enacts time's passing gestures

and the world glows with dull light;
a residue of thunder
coating the arrested air,
growing deeper, heavier.

I thought I'd got over this
but am grateful, all the same,
for love's return, another
round in an abandoned game;

grateful to find that the old
absurdly adolescent
symptoms of anxiety
are not wholly lost or spent,

and that long-discarded masks
seem homely, familiar –
forsaken melancholic,
ironic versifier …

But beyond the Anglepoise
the window holds dusk and rain
only just at bay and proves
Greville right: absence is pain.

Allotments at Baldock

Spilled out beyond the gasworks and the railway,
Scattered at random on the injured ground,
They lie, detached extensions of elsewhere,
Like amputated artificial limbs.

Potatoes, peas, broad beans, mad cabbages,
Eccentric uncut flowers which bloom to seed
Seek the embankment's gritty sanctuary
Or reappear among surprised backyards.

On unclaimed plots, an uninvited rash
Of poppies and, in crowded insolence,
Massed nettles, elder, hogweed, clematis
Proclaim a little civilisation's end.

From landlocked beach-huts, corrugated sheds,
Come sounds which seem obscurely nautical,
Marine metallic tinklings, and sad flags
To frighten off the doubtful inland birds.

Thus signalled is a patchwork of possession,
A borrowing unmortgaged, a free space
Devoutly Sunday-tended, reaffirming
Our weedy and tenacious-flowering grace.

Changing Trains

1. *Warren Street*

As Alice might have remarked:
I've fallen for it again.
The sign, as it always does,
Said 'Change at Warren Street';
But I know, I've always known,
It's quicker via Leicester Square.

Now acres of tiled burrow
Stretch out as I pad along,
Muttering 'warren, indeed'
And wondering dully where
Warren Street actually is.
I've never been up there.

2. *Charing Cross*

The trains of childhood: this is coming home.
For me '22' will always mean 'Hastings'
Or at least 'Not calling at London Bridge';
Nor New Cross, Hither Green and Elmstead Woods,
Still less at almost-fictive Chelsfield, where
My Sevenoaks tickets were always labelled 'via'.

Same sounds and smells, same diesel-tunnelled dirt,
Curtains (for wiping windows), bulbous lights …
An elderly lady sinks down opposite:
With resilient and grandmaternal pride,
'I've come all the way,' she sighs, 'from Bury St Edmunds.'
As if she'd walked; as if she'd reached an end.

Coda

Thelonious Monk, d. 17 February 1982

Goat-bearded, crazy-hatted old wrong-noter:
Your half-tones filled the gaps of adolescence,
When all brave young aficionados claimed
To know what you were up to: shameless bluff,
Until one day we woke to find it true.

Thus now hands, aimless on a keyboard, fall
Into 'Round Midnight' – haunted, audible
Through the sizzling of a Riverside EP
Those twenty years ago, the sheet music
Ordered from a baffled small-town shop:

Both still possessed, with later images
Of one March night in London, '65,
Prancing before a South Bank audience.
Within the pauses and abrasive chords,
Misterioso – hermit or buffoon?

No need to choose. I couldn't understand
Then how defences crowd about the self;
How, hedged around with paradox, we lose
The centre we defend; so couldn't know
Why you fragmented sentimental songs,

Invented notes for dislocated moods,
Evaded easy treasonable concord.
I'd hope but daren't believe at last you rest,
Beyond our life's perverse cacophony,
If not in peace, at least in harmony.

Citrus

If required to devise a desirable addiction,
    I would choose citrus.

Orange-juice, grapefruit coax the hungover soul
    To zestful good humour.

A messy selection of kitchen ingredients
    Is chastened by lemon.

Shades from pale lime to overripe orange
    Making waking worthwhile.

My desert island needs not only discs
    But these fruitful spheres.

July, 1982

Above, a hard untruthful sky
Denies all it has known of rain;
Outside, ill-tempered voices share
Irresolute, exhausted air
As summer closes in again,
And scandals, bombs and rumours fly.

Does nothing change? The words wear down:
Who claims responsibility;
The numbers dead; 'We will not rest
Until …'; the worst, the bloodiest;
Intelligence, security …
No words defuse when all is blown.

Days pass. The sky's blind perjuries
Reveal themselves: now dusk disturbs,
Arriving uninvited, wet,
And heavy through the distance lit
By flaring rosebay willow-herbs,
As summer storms among the trees.

Going Downhill

Head down, he crouches, almost quadruped,
Belly to earth and shoulders to the sun,
Above the speeding tubular machine,
So close it seems that he and it are one.

He travels with the gradient into shade.
The straight road dips through overarching trees:
Along his back, a sunlit silent film
Of switching patterns, boughs, translucent leaves.

Encased within a car, I envy that
Unfettered touch made bodily aware
Of every texture. Instinct angles him
For camber, curve: he challenges the air.

The slope runs out, he slows, I overtake –
A single pedal's pressure does the trick –
Then in the rear-view mirror, foot on brake,
Glimpse both a past self and a present fake.

In Arden: Cambridge, 1982

Phoebus Car: As You Like It

Space within space, fiction within fiction,
An evening bathed in melancholic light:
Through Petty Cury's sadly shuttered set
And Christ's linked courtyards, teasingly oblique,
To this squat shape of concrete and smoked glass;
Within, an empty unexpected space.

We enter in the self-regarding way
Small audiences have; converse a while;
Settle at length into the secure dark.
On stage, unlikely arguments commence,
Compelling younger brother, good old man,
Besotted cousins and bewildered clown
To leave for wintry Arden. They arrive;
Beguiled, as we are, by benevolence –
A vacant farm, food, hospitality,
The freedoms of delusion and disguise.

The season changes with the interval:
New leaves proclaim contingencies of spring,
Whose dance must undo mask and argument.
The wicked will be shown as merely dim,
The good as merely nice; and, as for us,
We have to choose our representative
And finally take sides: cynic or clown.

The Epilogue, a held half-open door,
Admits a chilling draught on what remains:
Exhausted players, artificial light,
And toyshop props of Touchstone's circus act –
Which recognition lengthens our applause
At their sustained improbability
Before we, Jaques-like, walk out on them.
This summer night holds no security.

Sleeper

At last, embattled sleep has locked you in
      Its stern repose;
Hardened against a world of love and doubt,
      Your body knows

A fortress strategy of self-defence;
      And yet, behind
The buttressed brow, that stray subversive dream
      Invades your mind.

There's nothing you can do to keep it out,
      For from the start
It's waited for the moment when the walls
      Will fall apart

To let in chaos, fragments of the void:
      They've got you now,
Until you wake, unfortified but strong
      With love, somehow.

Studies

for John Boumphrey

1. *Park Grange*

A dimly disinfected corridor
Leads back into the past, through ember light
From old bulbs nested in red plastic shades.
Its intersections tempt with dark dead ends:
Cracked and clattering pantry, endless cellar,
Deep cupboards housing colonies of shoes.
There's no escape nor whimsical detour.
The furniture of fear. The silent door.

2. *The Mews*

Trust's emblems: open doors, plain *Seniors*,
Freedom of uncharted bookshelves – this
Was all the world I wished to grow into.
Up skeletal boxed stairs to attic rooms
Where adolescent literati met
And unregarded age hung in the eaves:
Contained or cobwebbed by indifference,
We traded in our different innocence.

3. *The Well Cottage*

The six bells tumbled over misty elms
To summon the devout, unnoticing
A grey cat in the hedge, a dew-lit web
And a boy behind the leaded window, writing
At this desk, studious in another house.
I see him now, and want to say, 'Don't worry,
The years will heal your broken images.'
The whirligig of time brings his revenges.

4. *Kenilworth Road*

A midland window framed another view:
Suburban trees, back gardens, washing-lines
And afternoon sun sliced by venetian blinds.
Books, records, papers tried to lend a name
To stateless furniture: identities
Lodged tentatively in a no-man's land.
The sudden warmth of others: good to find
Such kindness shown to one not of their kind.

5. *Eastnor Grove*

An attic in a tall and silent house,
The wrong end of town, defining solitude:
I lived, consoled by anonymity,
For six safe months – deliberate prelude
To garret life, I thought. Enough of that:
Long evenings in the Roebuck; coming of age;
A few friends in the hazy rooms; below,
The trees in Eastnor Grove were hunched with snow.

6. *New Street*

The streetlamps flickered out in Distons Lane.
Above the arch, we played our dangerous game
Through smoky nights and aimless faded days,
Watching our selves or the receding room,
Booklined, Cotswold-stoned. It seemed enough:
Talk, music, whisky, dope, a little art,
Steps echoing in the archway; high above,
He said something or other about love.

7. *The Town*

A hamlet called The Town. And Matthew said,
'If I lived in a place like this, I'd write.'
We crossed the river meadows to the Crown,
Returning homeward through the mellow night,
Then talked on in the open-windowed room
Where honeysuckle weighed upon the air;
Knew nothing of the imminence of loss,
An accidental end, time's double-cross.

8. *Cambridge House*

Suddenly space: high ceilings and white walls.
Perhaps I thought a change would set me right –
Simple as that. False logic of façades,
An each-way bet, a love at second sight,
The liar's self-conviction of a truth:
Thus caution tempts desire to leasehold life.
Bland architectural graces, signs misread:
Within, some space stayed uninhabited.

9. *Church Street*

Now darkness has closed in around the desk.
The night's surviving colonists stand guard –
An angled lamp and a low-glowing fire
Where random bricks are blackened by old smoke.
Scotch, coffee, and the final Brandenburg:
At last a little time belongs to us.
Outside, the street is sobered, still: it's late.
The house's timbers gently ruminate.

So Much Unfinished

So much unfinished: rusty,
rakish, a garden fork stuck
by the cold sodden bonfire;
skirting-boards where undercoat
is coated only by dust;
stacked boxes in the attic,
packed at the move before last,
to sort out some rainy day.

Unanswerable letters.
'I just had to tell someone ...';
'You may not realise, but ...'
So much unburdened, so much
to share or to reassure:
terrors of being alone
or intrusive, insecure
mistrust of elders, betters.

And all happening again:
false signals, missed connections
where our separate regrets
die in their undue seasons.
So much unfinished, except
the ghost of an abruptly
fading farewell: the windswept
platform of a southbound train.

North Sea Nights

1

The last of sunlight lingers on the waves,
But suddenly the sea's not sociable:
The crowds have gone; it clears up after them,
Licks picnic remnants with a surly tongue,
Erodes their little moated monuments,
And scrambles all their sandy messages.
It dumps some salty oddments in exchange:
A bargain far from rich yet more than strange.

2

He comes in looking like the past he is.
Hello. We met before. Of course. A drink.
The jukebox plays the theme from something: strings
And soapy clarinet. 'I'm here all week –
The place I always stay when I'm this way.'
We share some snatched complicity, yet know
That after-closing-time will find me home,
Black coffee, the *Times* crossword, and alone.

3

'The Mass Orgie Shelter': so it's claimed
Below the coastguard station. Not tonight:
The entertainment's vanished under cover;
Puddles recall the high tide's hangover;
Misshapen Coke cans clog the gullies; light
Sweeps out from Orford Ness; while inland, high,
Five even-spaced red military lamps
Map out another world, scarring the sky.

4

'We're from Hemel.' Tattoos say he's Tony,
While she, not so announced, remains unnamed.
They're watchful, wide-eyed. 'They must do all right
Here,' he says, 'giving such short measure.' 'No,
Rather the reverse.' 'So that's it. Oh.'
'Try buying crisps or cigarettes, you'd find
They've "just sold out": it's always like that, yet
The place has something.' Yes. We drink to that.

5

Calm tonight: a footpath on the sea
To apricot moon, a little bruised, like me.

Coming to Light

They're faint at first, watermarks
in grey antique laid paper,
apparent indentations
in the fabric of the air;

then, gently liberated
from river-mist, they reveal
themselves as masts, truncated
by harbour or by sea-wall;

and strangely, as detail grows,
the newly-defined appear
less real – dull purplish mallows
turn luminous, and the near

masts are hardening to black
snappable twigs, transient,
about to shatter or crack.
What's well lit is too present:

it's others, coming to light,
contain both future and past,
held at the limits of sight,
claimed by and claiming the mist.

Listening to Rain

'How often have I lain beneath rain on a strange roof, thinking of home.'
William Faulkner, As I Lay Dying

There were nights I'd lie awake, listening to rain
Shuddering on slates or tickling the gutter:
Nights when the universe was rain-defined,
Gaps padded with moisture, and the space
Between here and there confined within a shower.
Nearby cars were slurring round a corner
On the road home: I'd think of warm interiors,
Green glow of dashboards, air soft with tobacco,
Relaxed hands on wheels, and desultory chatter
Of those who know they'll get to where they're going.

So, there were nights: and even now I'd feel
Abrupt chilled air of a winter dormitory,
Sash windows open, curtainless, bare floor,
An iron bedstead's knotty skeleton.
Fitzgerald said it's always three o'clock
In the dark night of the soul; for me it was
Round midnight, which bewitching time intrudes,
My friend, on different myths – truncated times

Snatched from us on wet garden city streets,
Or gusty emotions in the empty early hours.

Now raindrops on a skylight merge, diverge,
Form tributaries towards the imminent sea
Which in some sunny elsewhere you're beyond:
On Rhodes it seems it's 32°,
And that at least's unenvied; while outside,
The space expands to claim a galaxy,
Inhuman and unbridgeable, where lights,
Flickering on a further shore, are doused
By absences, departures, nights I've lain
Beneath a strange roof, listening to rain.

Outside

Outside, on the veranda, chairs and table,
Their white paint pimpled by autumnal rust:
Two glasses and a cracked decanter proffer
A static invitation, an old trust.

Here change is texture and decay is growth:
The boards no longer creak, a fine silt seals
These soft interstices whose grains play host
To tawny mosses; every plank conceals

Communities of woodlice. At the edge,
A deckchair's frame surveys the wilderness
Of reedy water, tattered canvas flags,
Loose pages of the *Eastern Daily Press*;

And late sun seeps to the veranda, where
It lights, like the bright future, on a chair.

Raw

All day I've felt raw. My head's
Like a cheap radio off-station –
Fading thin whistle, white noise;
My eyes graze in sandpaper sockets.

All's suddenly heavy, ill-fitting:
I'm carrying a stranger around,
Unsure where I picked him up
Or whose weary limbs I have found.

Perhaps that's what age is: growing
Unfit and unfitted, until
The furniture starts to attack –
Your favourite chair wrecks your back.

The rain's stopped: out in the street,
The lights have come on and the young
Saunter by. I make for the door:
There are more kinds of folly than one.

Distant Music

Across hot roofs and unfamiliar streets
Comes distant music: honed by stone and slates
Into angular shapes, it pulses, demanding
Allegiance. The piper, unpied, unyielding,
Stands on a wide white balcony, beyond
The dry contingent thoroughfare: around
This corner, up these narrow steps, and on
Through blistered high-walled alleys where the sun
Dips warily and only at midday.

The sound commands; the listeners obey.

At last, beyond the railings, he is there,
In faded denim, faded yellow hair,
Charming the alto sax whose gold has won
The modest light and claimed it for its own.
It utters now an endless twining riff
That Charlie Parker played, glinting as if
The sound were light refracted and elsewhere
Returned to what it was, a part of air.

The boy has paused for breath: he stares, intent,
Perplexed and rueful, at his instrument,
As if he knows his ariel charm must vanish
Or that he too, out on the street, will tarnish.

Therfield

We sit outside, as dusk falls, with our beers.
Mine tastes autumnal: mist and smoke unfold
On cue from gardens round the village green
And shadowed lanes. The summer has grown old.

We watch the long perspective – walls and hedges
End in a distant gable – and imagine
How there we might inhabit quiet lives.
I dare not say you have no place in mine.

Natural Magic

He arrives, from studio or surf,
It doesn't matter which,
In racing shorts and sailing top.
Half the bar falls instantly in love.
Blond, chunky, looks sixteen,
He must be all of twenty-five:
He's wonderfully preserved.

Perfect strangers soon believe
They're among his oldest friends:
He knows everyone, chats to some,
Drinks could it be lager?
You smile: pure apple juice,
Never touches alcohol,
And, oh no, no preservative.

True Colours

Today the sea is the colour of the sky,
And neither is blue. But look, at the water's edge,
There's a girl in a blossoming yellow anorak;
By her, an ultramarine man. She is the colour
Of a plausible buttercup, and he …
                                   They are watching,
Attentively following something I cannot see,
Until at last a sudden tiny child
Springs, as it seems, from the shingle in the drizzle,
Clutching an orange polygon.
                              Impossibly,
The kite flies, darts like a drunk insect, crashes
Abruptly onto an astonished patchwork dog.
A matching gull flaps by, huge, out of scale.

Or so, surely, it was. For, turning again
To the rainswept window, I find that they
Have all moved out of frame. All that remain
Are the true colours: mutual, neutral grey.

My Father's Business

'And if they ask you what you're going to do,
Just say, "My father's business".' Kind advice,
From hard-won pride: I memorised the phrase.
The school gave me, though not for that, a place.

It seemed a fiction: shambling trolleybuses
In Charterhouse Street's perennial peopled gloom;
The brave new *Mirror* building taking shape;
Old leather chairs, a dark partitioned room,

Black bulbous phones, perpetual calendars,
A working space contained and carpeted.
I'd have liked to meet his cronies at the Mitre,
But was too young. We lunched at the Globe instead.

My father had skate: I watched him closely.
His needs – fish, beer, the business – were precise:
In charge, as I am now, of a chosen world,
He gained an unexpected gentle ease.

'Very nice.' He paid. Then back to the office:
The stairwell drenched in underwater light,
Diagonal gilt lettering on glass,
And distant steps of other business feet.

His co-director, stately and severe,
Behind a frosted door, Miss Warmington,
Who had no first name or other existence,
Fulfilled some secret, necessary function.

Across the corridor, the showroom glowed:
Glass lit through glass, a churchlike radiance,
Refracting samples of a crystal world.
One day it would all be mine? No chance.

I couldn't play the boss's son. I'd phone,
Irresolutely, Holborn 9622.
'Would you put me through to Mr Powell?'
'Who's calling?' 'Er, it's Neil.' 'Neil who?'

I could have told them then it wouldn't do.

Visiting

Those houses are too square, those roads too straight,
And the trees, though old, look planted to conceal
Some sheltered institution – hospital
Or army base. We find the visitors' gate:
A car-park conifered as a cemetery,
Well-ordered, clean. You'd know it miles away.

Now, like all guilty secrets, it unmasks
Its human face: a shabby hall set out
With coffee, tea, as for a village fête;
Familiar transactions, social tasks
In a world removed from all we could transact;
And people round us trying to connect

The outside past – 'Do you remember?' – to this,
The present, inside. Lives have raced ahead
On different tracks, with so much left unsaid,
And now unsayable, that we dismiss
The normal words: gossip, solemnity
Seem to affront the occasion equally.

'It won't be long.' The parting sounds inane.
'We'd better let you out,' the warders smile:
The trees, of course, were planted to console.
They fail. The landscape opens once again –
A low green wood, shut pubs, a water tower –
And freedom, if that is what this is, tastes sour.

III

1987–1997

Sun Street

1

A boy walks past. He's wearing faded jeans
And a garish big-checked peppermint-green shirt.
The clash is vivid and familiar:
You wore, a dozen years ago, the same
Woeful mix. I thought you colour-blind,
Or maybe just revered your recklessness;
But that was in another summer, and
Mortality is standing in the way.

2

'All right, all right,' he drawls as he walks away.
He looks like something out of *My Beautiful Laundrette*.
'You bastard,' she yells. 'I'll kill you.' 'All right, all right.'
Milk bottles smash. A child screams. And a dog,
Parked in an expensive car, yaps plaintively.

I was brooding on some niggling misery
When that little scene occurred to cheer me up.
Catharsis is too grand a word for it:
Just good to know that frustration, anger, pain
Aren't exclusively owned. On the absurd chimney
Above the butcher's shop, a blackbird calls curfew.

3

The dry-cleaner's son is ruining my life.
Two years ago, he'd help out Saturdays,
Slight boyish chores rewarded with ice-cream.

Last summer, he'd grown lanky, self-aware:
Out in the street, washing his father's van,
They staged a grand balletic water-fight.

Now, taller of the two, he calls me 'mate',
Will deputise for dad, or join him in
A loose bravado, male confederacy.

His shirts – today, gigantic hippie flowers –
Are as loud as his crotch-line; and his former selves
Lost postcards from the summers left behind.

The Difference

for Adam Johnson

We watch the gathering sea through sepia dusk
Across a beach of fish-heads, glass beads, relics
Dumped by a careless deity called chance.
Ferry and trawler exchange a passing glance.

Dark comes fast: lighthouse and streetlamp pierce it.
You sit at the window, silent as I write.
We are no longer locked in self-defence.
Being with you has made all the difference.

The Lunatics' Compartment

A Courtly Epistle for A.J.

It's England, nineteen-eighty-eight.
The rain comes on, the train comes late.
I choose the lunatics' compartment:
In front, a snow-thatched don, intent
On squinting back across his seat;
Behind, protruding trainered feet,
A stoned recumbent boy, half-dressed,
Prompts academic interest.

At Finsbury Park, the spiral stairs
Are urinous as ever: there's
The rumble of the train I've missed;
Two Irishmen, already pissed,
Dispute the time. Three stations on,
A grinning beefy lad gets on:
His left leg pressed on my right, he
Checks out desire's seismology.

Next into Thresher's in Earl's Court,
Seeking the dry white I'd want brought
To my own party. Outside, it's
Time to give thanks for leather jackets:
I sprint off down the rain-surged street,
Pass John Heath-Stubbs and know we'll meet
In Redcliffe Gardens, think about
Just one in the Coleherne? Better not.

Inside the hall, we greet and kiss.
You say, 'We don't usually do this
When we meet in London.' And that's so,
But here it's suddenly as though
We're self-enclosed if not alone.
A naked boy is on the phone,

And from an open door drift through
Camp music and a voice or two.

The room's embalmed from nineteen-ten:
Old furniture, old books, old men,
And now an odd perception, which is
Candles here have dimmer switches.
The wine is white and warm and sweet,
The chatter joylessly discreet;
No intellectual risks are taken
Until … of course, it's Eddie Linden.

Enters mid-sentence, going on
About getting mugged in Paddington,
Which makes him now, amazingly,
Sober and plastered, as if he
Is London: walking-wounded place
Whose gracefulness is in disgrace,
Whose refugees are gathered here,
The brave and literate and queer.

The naked boy, now dressed, is an
Escapee from the Barbican:
He looks around this courtly scene,
Unsure but every inch a queen,
Creating little waves of truth
As each of us recalls his youth
Or wonders who will take the plunge
And make some sad nostalgic lunge.

Elsewhere Hugh David talks about
The English Gentleman, that lout
On whom he's writing; Francis King
Decides to tango, though nothing
Seems (luckily) to come of it;
And I remember Michael Schmidt
At Earl's Court Square: 'We're getting old:
You've grown eyebrows, I've gone bald.'

It's not my scene, I guess, and so
At ten o'clock I turn to go:
I use as my excuse a train
Though feel the pull of bars and rain.
A cinematic staircase kiss
Brings its lovely echo, this:
The poem, not our love, is finished;
I would not have that love diminished.

Poet and Pheasant, Totleigh Barton

All week, I've tried to put your words on my page –
And mine, I fear, on yours. Before you wake,
I walk in search of the single snapshot image:
Mist-brimming fields, perhaps, or sudden sunlight
Shearing through trees to light upon the village;
A pheasant choking on the edge of utterance.

Strangeways

'Hooded rioters, a noose hanging from a pillar, appeared on the roof yesterday with a possible hostage. The man's hands are bound, and he seemed to be being threatened with a carving knife.'

Caption in The Independent, *4 April 1990*

These hooded gestures look familiar
From mutilated statues, gargoyles,
Dark icons of forgotten underworlds.
The fork is from the cutlery of hell,
Portending some slow medieval death.
One pallid central figure clasps bound hands
In slack, uncertain attitude of prayer:
His level gaze is sculpted as a mask,
His arms bulked out of all proportion,
Carved limbs upon an aristocratic tomb.
They stand, the three of them, against scarred arches;
Another lurks beyond the churchly pillars,
Attending to a noose.
                This is our time:
Each culture gets the myths that it deserves.

You've Changed

S.L., 1990

I looked, of course, across a crowded bar,
Admired at once the perfect sense of poise,
Deep chestnut eyes, abruptly squared-off jaw,
Which made you so much more than pretty. Days

Passed uncounted, months, and maybe years
Until that Sunday evening when I saw
You sitting at a table in the garden,
Dalton's Weekly and a drink beside you.

'You look like something out of Graham Greene,'
I said absurdly, meaning I suppose
You had the air of an expatriate.
I might have put it otherwise: 'You've changed.'

Immeasurable, the distance that can pass
Across a glass, and then another glass:
The truths and reckless confidence exchanged
As a long evening grows to over-late.

No real surprise to see the cracks appear.
We knew them all along: the tear, the scar
Which makes us so much more than perfect, through
A lifetime spent on books and booze and boys,

On things that were, or even things that are.

In Another Light

Not even sun's false innocence
Can cover this: smaller today,
The island finds its boundaries,
Flexes as the tide subsides
And waves bathe other surfaces.

I share the land's astonishment
At the beach's lowered profile:
Planed to pebble-smoothness,
Uneasy in its changed shape,
It mutters, rattles, settles.

Gulls discover new salt lakes
Among the silent, stoic cows;
Beyond the damp seaweedy sand
Which marks the ocean's last advance,
The shingle ridge has rolled inland.

The surge spent, in another light
Storm dwindles into memory,
And children from the local school
Scatter the débris of the night,
Revising their geography.

The End of Summer

I close my eyes. There's a knotty apple-tree,
Grasped to a landscaped lawn, its fruit unripe;
A Labrador, greying at the jowls, asleep;
My mother, gently stabbing at the crossword
With mild success; my father is at work.

I am at home now, but not for long.
My imagination is going to take me away.
Things are about to change: I've heard rumours,
Like odd creaks on the stairs, while I'm in bed
Fading in tune with Radio Luxembourg.

We've been to get my new school uniform
At the outfitters: a sombre narrow shop,
Innocent of daylight or fresh air,
With a sombre narrow man who peered at me
As if I wasn't quite their class of boy.

'Still in short trousers' means just what it says:
'Only rough boys wear jeans.' Long trousers now;
My mother sews in Cash's woven name-tapes
While I watch *Juke Box Jury*. Ding! A hit!
I've seen the future and he's called Craig Douglas.

I pass whole days in an ecstasy of growing,
This wonderful summer: I empathise with plants –
Beans running, bamboo shooting, even the bees
Have somehow heard a buzz and are on the scent.
I know more than could possibly be good for me.

The stillness of held breath is on the air,
While thunder gathers in the wings of autumn.
I know high cloud will slowly bleach the sky,
Leaves turn to russet, late apples ripen,
And light will never be quite like this again.

The Stones on Thorpeness Beach

for Guy Gladwell

O luminosity of chance!
Light spins among the spider-plants
As sand or amber glow seeps through
Tall windows of a studio,
While on the beach in random rows
The enigmatic stones compose
A silent staveless variation,
The music of regeneration.

Relearn astonishment, and see
Where splinters of eternity
Still glitter at the water's edge,
Beyond the tideline's daily dredge
Of flotsam: plants and creatures who'd
Survive this stale decaying world,
And stones worn smooth as solid tears,
Each crafted by a million years.

Or dusky rain across the sea,
Dull pewter light, when suddenly
The level sun breaks through, makes clear
Another perfect hemisphere:
Its rainbow-self, supported by
A dark horizon, arcs the sky.
I watch the colours falter and,
Slipping on shingle, fall on sand.

Yet, high above the crumbling cliff,
A concrete pillbox stands as if
In crazy gesture of defence;
As if the huge indifference
Of change, decay, might somehow be
Perturbed by such small dignity
Which slowly shifts and cracks, and so
Will shatter on the stones below.

Search for a sound hypothesis:
'Safe as houses', 'Bank on this',
Dead clichés of security!
Houses? Bank? You'd better tie
Mementoes in a plastic bag,
Chuck in the sea, mark with a flag
The spot where fish or mermen may,
With luck, remember you one day.

Our rented time is running out,
But unlike tide won't turn about
With regular and prompt dispatch
To land upon the beach fresh catch,
As gradually, with gathering pace,
Life ebbs out from the human race
Inhabiting a world grown ill.
Time for a benediction still.

Peace to the gulls and guillemots,
To curlews and their bleak mudflats,
To sea-birds, sea-anemones,
To marsh-plants, meadow butterflies,
To lavender and gorse and mallows,
To creatures of the depths and shallows;
Peace to the vast blue out-of-reach;
Peace to the stones on Thorpeness Beach.

A Virus

The words won't scan. Initials, acronyms
Are tidier though no less threatening:
They claim it for bureaucracy, as if
Depriving it of an imaginary life.

I try: I sense it crazily adrift
On a wild surge of involuntary current,
Like the lost boat in a forgotten nursery rhyme.
It had no choice in the matter, meant no harm.

But see how it turns our calm world upside-down!
Your comical pill-popping hypochondria
Seems mere rehearsal for reality,
Your lithe past an irrational vanity.

So now your boast is: 'Look, I've put on weight.'
Your breakfasting on booze has given way
To healthy muesli, yoghurt, wholemeal bread,
Storing up strength for the wasted days ahead.

Providence

The Providence Baptist Chapel, Aldringham,
Is light industrial: factory for souls.
Abandoned among heather, fern and gorse,
Where birches lean their leaves against the wind,
It prompts old questions. Why here? Why at all?
I half-admire that monstrous confidence,
Unthinking certainty of doing good,
Which dumped a bumptious bright-red pantiled barn
Out here, far from community and road.

Now broken-windowed, boarded and patrolled
(It says) by ghostly guard-dogs, Providence
Has fallen out of use.
                              Young oaks surprise
And jostle through the rusted graveyard fence.
The loyal congregation, being dead –
Adah Cadey, Sam Studd, Jabez Bird –
Worship in green, while yellow daisies dance
Upon the grave of Percy Marjoram,
Tended with love's defiance.
                              I walk on,
Along a sandy track, a silent lane:
New planting, like a wartime cemetery
Or rockets poised for launch on Guy Fawkes' Night,
Proclaims the former forest's greener hope;
And a neat brick row of charitable homes
Shows how goodwill can be inhabited
As peace of mind, as warmth.
                              Yet faith runs cold.
A sign outside the Baptist Chapel said:
Black Horse Agencies (Subject to Contract) SOLD.

Aubergines

After hours, off-duty, the young chef talks:
He perches, in his denim earnestness,
On a bar-stool, folds himself like an omelette,
And worries about his troubles with aubergines.

There are times to be not a fly on the wall,
Nor in the soup, but a kind ironic god:
Invisible, I watch the two of you press on
Through the whole ratatouille of emotion.

Borodins and Vodka

for Dmitri Shebalin

A resident quartet.
A form of words, and yet
Through catastrophic days
This bleak eroded coast
Provides, as it has done
Before, safe anchorage.
Resident: at worst,
Administrative fiction;
At best, true habitation,
Huge vodkas in the Keys.

There's something in the air
Of Suffolk-Russian kinship:
How many programmes pair
Britten-Shostakovich.
And Ben's interpreters:
Richter, Rostropovich.
A chill from the sea, perhaps;
The windy never-stillness
Impels us to create
Our best, our better-than.

Evenings we'll not forget:
That January storm
Percussed the Maltings roof
(Tchaikovsky 3 beneath);
Fine Easter miniatures
Or summer Russian masters
With family connections
In eloquent sonatas;
A form of words, and yet
A resident quartet.

True Stories

A Little Rain or Drizzle

Sun, you see: sun's unreality
Flooding the smudged surfaces of life.
All's reinvented, clean; but there may be
A little rain or drizzle before dusk.

Poetry Society

Tonight an evening for the little poets,
There being no big poets left alive.
The reader carries a speech impediment,
The chairman a handbag. I'm wondering
How to persuade the peanuts along the bar.

Base Boys

They lounge around the share-a-ride layby
Like almost ordinarily aimless lads,
Ill-fitted in their clothes, yet can't disguise
Bad haircuts, shiny features, nervous eyes.
The grid of buildings, service roads could be
A campus: University of War.
They learn jokes here: 'Why's Saddam Hussein
Like a pair of tights?' 'They both' –
The unblushing answer – 'irritate Bush.'
The School of Politics is strong
On economy of language. 'Man,' he says,
'We're going to *concrete* Iraq.'

Michael Laskey on a Bicycle

Hatted and scarfed as a red Christmas card,
He pedals down Main Street, like in a movie,
Because in Leiston, it has to be said,
There's nothing you could call seriously High.

How Are You Today?

Dear Peter Barker: I could take
The progress of roses with Patricia Hughes;
Tom Crowe's mistakes; or even Donald Price
Refusing to read a story in the news.
But what the waking soul cannot endure is:
'This is Peter Barker opening up
Radio 3, *and how are you today*?'

Look

Just one look, just like the song,
That's all it took, and here I am again,
Anguishing by my Anglepoise lamp again,
Waiting for open bars, open arms, open.

Yoggit

They call him Yoggit, because he says,
'I always has yoggit for me tea.'
Watches the fight, then shadow-boxes,
Punching grey air. 'Go on, Yoggit.'
He dances, punishes the empty space,
Sees shadows, but these pensioners are real.

Neil's Yard

It's anarchy out there: nicotiana
Stoned out of their flowery heads;
Ivy-leaved pelargoniums
Gone woodily assertive; and beans,
Up the wall, over the roof ...

It's hard to keep up: I rescue fronds
Of lolling Chilean glory vine
(And end of course by snapping them);
Winged purple bells downturned,
Fuchsias in suspended mid-dive ...

And then the welcome invaders:
Poppies, toadflax, yellow vetch,
Lobelia – all self-seeded hangers-on ...
A boudoir for bees, an aphids' banquet:
What god of paradox has made this place?

Crane-flies and Dragon-flies

September, and the coastal insect life
Is reinvented by Heath Robinson:
Crane-flies dangle by spare limbs from webs
Or land on sand to drown in the next wave;
Above the abandoned railway-track inland,
Bright dragon-flies like airshow prototypes
Fly stunts among the berries, fading blooms.

King's Cross

There are things which I cannot determine, even on good days.
Why is the open-door-button a breast in a mortuary?
How did today's ticket sneak to the back of my wallet?
Why do I always end up in the lunatics' coach?

Mr Gadget

Today he's mending Charlotte's typewriter,
And tinkering with another vintage car,
While planning his next essay on aesthetics
(Holding ideas up in his hands like bricks).

Tonight he'll lurk, webbed in his special corner,
And contemplate the boys along the bar;
His dreams are coated with procrastination
(It's just an act of the imagination).

Gulls

'Boat ashore 3.30 – 4. pm.'
These seawise birds know better:
The clamorous mob escorts it in,
Sharper than starlings, hardly gullible.

Inland

The summer's burden turns to benediction.
Softened by sudden warmth, the leaves relax
And rest upon the breeze. We should have known
That this was what we wanted all along.

A Photograph of Thomas Mann

You remember the one.
It's on the back of fifties Penguins.

The pen's held at an angle of thought:
Or second-thought, proof-correction.

The mouth's a mere line of contained
Amusement, self-deprecation.

And the veined warty face tells of age,
Its age: when writers

Wore sombre spectacles, bankers' suits,
And dignity, and hope.

George

I'd say no pub's complete without its George –
Crabby, cantankerous, in a corner near the bar.
One was stone-deaf, looked like Sibelius;
Another had his own stool, bottle, glass;
But only you were Irish too. So when
An overdressed woman's pampered poodle trod
On your foot, you growled: 'You fucking stupid bitch.'
'He isn't,' she snapped primly, 'he's a dog.'
'I wasn't,' you said, 'referring to the dog,'
And rearranged the contours of your face,
Sniffing a bit, yet radiant with gin.

The Gift

All we have is all we have to say,
Unless the gift becomes a giveaway.

The Reasonable Shore

Their understanding
Begins to swell, and the approaching tide
Will shortly fill the reasonable shore,
That now lies foul and muddy.

Shakespeare, The Tempest

And there are days, beyond dog-days of summer,
When the restless ocean gathers in repose,
Soughing and lapping at unprinted sand,
Proving that greatest power is power contained.

Shakespeare's shore of reason was the mind
Which, he believed, the tide would cleanse and fill
With water's bright lucidity. How could
A dark intelligence hold such faith in good?

The mirror-sea, example and reproach,
In each return confounds the cankered past
And leaves a world renewed with each withdrawal
(Though that is not what Shakespeare meant at all).

Sixpence for the Man

Two silver coins in penny-farthing scale:
'Half a crown, and sixpence for the man.'
Leon Molin: front a chemist's shop.
The room beyond seemed subterranean:
Oblique light from a garden, fishtank-green.

The sharp, specific foreignness of things:
Floor-standing ashtrays, chromium-plated shrubs
With hungry bulbous roots; bright flasks of 'spray';
Loose stacks of *Titbits*, *Picture Post*, *Reveille*;
A hatstand with more hats than customers.

Waiting my turn, I'd try to calculate
Which one I'd get: the white-haired on the left,
A kindly grandfather I'd never known,
Or the smart schoolmasterly bully on the right,
Glancing at me archly: 'Next, young man!'

At home my father sometimes washed my hair
In glutinous amber shampoo: 'Soup!' he'd call,
As my dripping scalp emerged from its solution
Of Nucta Oil, brand from the gullible past,
Like Kolynos toothpaste, verdant chlorophyll –

Obtainable, no doubt, from Leon Molin.
Yet I'll retain my vexed embarrassment
At one shy boy's charade of confidence,
And two old barbers, threatening and mild,
Meekly accepting pennies from a child.

Moving House

'This is a dream,' I tell myself, waking,
'And what it is says isn't real.' But there's my house,
Its stairs and its ramshackle rooms overflowing
With people from the street, and that blonde girl you knew.

I've really no idea what they're all doing there,
This whole vacant parade of the unwanted world.
Now we've found our own space, so I no longer care:
Released from your wrapping, you are my present.

Yet what subtle adjustments we've made since we began
To know each other last winter: I've even grown to love
Those dead flattened vowels you claim as Australian.
Holding you now, I could tear you apart like bread.

My head on your musky chest, I must have slept,
Waking to find the house still crowded, its furniture
Dispersed and rearranged, all out of place except
You, warm in weak sunlight on your nest of denim.

I cautiously explore: a pine table from the kitchen
Is wedged into the study, whose papers and books
Are strewn in the bathroom, my history rewritten
By strangers who view me with unconcerned reserve.

And here's the blonde girl, perched on the landing,
Leaning on a sideboard I've never seen before.
'I told you he wasn't like that,' she says, smiling.
'Oh, but' – I'm smiling too – 'he is. He is.'

Two Rollerskaters in Oakley Square

Like evening gnats these adolescents find
    An island of late sunlight
To turn and circle in, and to unwind
    Their tangled day to night.

The dark plump one makes his agility
    Appear a conjuring trick:
A purple sphere, it's marvellous that he
    Can twist and spin and flick

His ankles over pavement-edge or grating;
    Ends vindicate his means.
Beyond, his friend comes, slyly hesitating
    In faded sawn-off jeans,

Bleached spiky hair, precisely ripened tan,
    Wide-striding sinewy grace:
He wears his body almost like a man,
    Choosing new movements, new pace.

For Music

1

It's a genuine sense of my own unworthiness
that's made me delay this thank-you letter for so long,
      and I still feel nervous about beginning,
            as if our steady affair is less

a relationship than a consequence of being –
born in misunderstanding, like all biographies –
      or else an intrusion on family ties
            too intimate and too far-reaching

for me to tangle with. Your shadier relatives,
encountered long ago, in strange and shady places,
      mustn't be denied their proletarian graces
            which may, after all, have shaped our lives:

like tough boys in the playground, whose threats were promises,
they tattooed their names on a child's imagination –
      Paul Anka, Elvis Presley, Frankie Lymon
            and (O brave new word) The Teenagers –

so much packed in the emblems of a generation,
such confidence that we were the first who'd ever heard,
      that soon we'd even swoon over Cliff Richard.
            No doubt it's a shaming admission

if I confess I never liked the stuff but wanted
(as with film-stars, footballers) to have one of my own,
      or get in on the act myself. Thus began
            the world's worst pop group, and thus ended:

no harm in that, beyond embarrassment and broken
guitar-strings; as painless a way as we could manage
      to skid through adolescent rites of passage,
          though clearly it couldn't last. By then,

I'd fallen for jazz, that potent echo of an age
just past, experience just missed, yet surviving
      for the dusty, smoky moment: hours browsing
          in Dobell's basement among vintage

78s, and enraptured evenings listening
to visiting Americans, Monk or Ellington
      playing 'Round Midnight' or 'In a Mellotone'
          live in London – it don't mean a thing

if it ain't got that swing … Would you believe I even
wrote a monthly column for the *Daily Telegraph*
      as a 'Young Critic': took it on for a laugh,
          the records, and for Philip Larkin,

who did their proper reviews and so chose my stuff –
a kindly, sad man I'm glad in the end to have met.
      Meanwhile, formed almost the world's worst jazz quartet,
          proved that devotion isn't enough,

despite Pee Wee Thornton on alto and clarinet
(the John Coltrane of New South Wales), and two more cronies
      stretched past the limit of their abilities;
          Tirez (however) *le pianiste!*

You see, Music, I'd a simple trick to learn, which is:
work at your second love, and keep your first well guarded;
      that's why I'm hunched over this sort of keyboard
          and not the illusive ivories.

2

I owe a surprising debt to Mr Collingwood,
who taught some odds and ends of English to the sixth form:
      one dozy afternoon in the autumn term,
            finding his class strangely depleted

by illness or excursion, he took the remnants home
to his flat across the High Street, bribed us with coffee,
      played a record of the Orchestral Suite in B
            minor by Bach. It worked like a charm,

works still (for heaven's sake): it's strange how momentously
the certainty struck that this was the stuff after all,
      and that it was almost inexhaustible,
            centuries of it stored up for me.

The road to Damascus? Well, nearly. Unlike St Paul,
what I'd stumbled to was addition, not conversion:
      for this was the mid-sixties, spinning on
            the kaleidoscopic musical

merry-go-round that drove The Beatles' revolution,
though it had hardly started. True, they'd topped the charts and
      even been taken seriously, had earned
            famous praise from the *Times'* William Mann

while delirious Beatlemania swept the land,
but so much of the best was still to come: *Revolver*,
      'Penny Lane' and 'Strawberry Fields Forever';
            Sgt Pepper's Lonely Hearts Club Band.

Thus some gullible critics began to consider
a grand reunion of your scattered family,
      including the freaks, all living happily
            in peace, brotherhood, etcetera;

so Maxwell Davies arranged McCartney's 'Yesterday'
(as if it needed it), and there was David Bedford
     hopping between the Soft Machine and the Third,
        and The Who with a piece called *Tommy*,

which they claimed was 'rock opera', and nobody laughed.
But meanwhile your poor relations were breeding again,
     poorer, meaner than ever, punkishly vain,
        leaving the sixties gratefully dead.

3

My formative Bach was pre-authentic: Menuhin
in boxy suites with the Bath Festival Orchestra,
     or with George Malcolm in the odd sonata;
        the Pears/King's College *St John Passion*;

and astonishing bargains – Harry Newstone's Saga
LPs of the *Brandenburgs*, Martin Galling's *Goldberg
     Variations*, ubiquitous Württemberg
        Chamber Orchestra, Segovia

and Rosalyn Tureck on a blurred ten-bob bootleg.
Sturdy, eternal vinyl, they travelled beside me
     through nomadic student days to provide me
        with pleasure and a musical peg

to hang my ideals on when the world rocked too wildly.
Hence the harsh injunction to descend a semitone,
     to relish scrapes and scratches of a hard-won
        warts-and-all originality

didn't seem an unfettered blessing nor was it one:
for Harnoncourt and Hogwood and Parrott and Pinnock
     (the latter in that ludicrous rustic smock)
        brought restoration, revelation,

heightened contrasts as a protecting veil was thrown back;
yet the result was uncomfortable, like living
      in a freshly spring-cleaned room, somehow wanting
          to turn down the contrast, smudge the black

and glacial white. I remember disagreeing
about not Bach but *Dido and Aeneas*, damned by
      choosing Janet Baker, not Emma Kirkby,
          unrepentant and unrepenting.

4

It's sad that certainties fell so unhelpfully
out of favour (on Radio 3 some smug buffoon
      just now said: 'No one believes in the canon
          any more'), for self-evidently

Dido and Aeneas makes an excellent touchstone:
whichever way we cast our vote, we'll have to admit
      that our desert island must have room for it,
          and that uncommitted abstention

would be unforgivable. Music, it's your habit
to make us disputatious: think how passionately
      I'll argue the merits of Gerald Finzi,
          Samuel Barber, Michael Tippett,

the off-centre romantics true to our century;
or how ruthlessly deride my cranky aversions,
      Brahms, Chopin, Liszt. Such harmless diversions
          clutter the central issue, namely

you've provided some transmogrifying occasions –
the first encounters with Shostakovich or Britten
      or Mahler, composers who've somehow grown
          to become components, possessions,

bits of the inmost self. 'And if you could take just one?'
(Whatever, you'd grow to loathe it, the question's crazy.)
        Well, it has to be Mahler, it has to be
              Simon Rattle, his *Resurrection*.

5

Out here in East Anglia, we're in a sense lucky:
we've one of the loveliest concert halls in the land
        (though some of the dimmest audiences) and
              the power of chance or destiny

has blessed it. Between works, between August storms, to stand
as liquid-patterned starlings flock above the reed-beds,
        against the dusk, as distant lightning recedes
              over the dark sea, and as inland

a clearing evening sky turns luminous blue and floods
the landscape with unearthly brilliance … this, Music,
        is beyond even your transforming magic,
              though comprehended in your concords.

But if that conceit's a shade Pythagorean, take
a different meshing of art and geography:
        in Britten I always hear the howling sea,
              its intermittent calm and sharp break

over the stony ridge; and it's there, obsessively,
not just in *Peter Grimes*, but a constant shifting ground
        (no paradox to those who live within sound
              of Aldeburgh beach); inevitably,

in the intricate transactions of tides, shingle, sand,
there's a music perpetually changing, renewing.
        So now a disc of Pogorelich playing
              early Haydn, making it new-found,

as it always is and must be, nudges at something
we might have guessed all along: that to rediscover
is the only true discovery, that our
necessary task is remaking

the fractured past. In dislocated times, whenever
our lives are uncertain and our best words meaningless,
you nourish us with coherence and wholeness.
Music, may you flourish for ever.

Outing

Who's leading this procession, then?
Peter Pears and Baron Britten,
Freddie Ashton, Wystan Hugh
Auden and Herr Issyvoo,
E.M. Forster, E.F. Benson,
Angus Stewart, Angus Wilson,
John Gielgud, Joe Ackerley,
Peter Ilyich Tchaikovsky,
Patrick Procktor, Derek Jarman,
Michael Leonard, Michael Cashman,
David Leavitt, David Hockney,
David Rees, Paul Gambaccini,
Peter Tatchell, Peter Burton,
Boy outside without a shirt on
(Wishful thinking), Andy Bell,
Neil Tennant, Jimmy Somerville,
Francis Poulenc, Edward Lucie-
Smith, Pier Paolo Pasolini,
Stephen Gilbert, Samuel Barber,
Peter Robins, Adam Mars-Bar,
Duncan Campbell, Jason who?
(Not *that* one, he'd only sue),

Desmond Hogan, Ian Charleson,
Marc Almond, er-Tom Robinson,
Thom Gunn, John Ash, Ian McKellen,
Alan Hollinghurst, Ned Sherrin,
Nick de Jongh, Chris Smith, Ray Gosling,
Matthew Parris, Francis King,
Kit Marlowe though alas Shakespeare
Wasn't *absolutely* queer,
Jeremy Beadle, Jeremy
Reed, Jules Clary, Tennessee
Williams, Oscar Wilde, Rock Hudson,
Michael Mason, Michael Nelson,
Nelson's chef Shane, Noel Coward,
Philip Ridley, Frankie Howerd,
James Baldwin, Kirkup, Dean, just James …
Enough of regimented names.
That wasn't too exciting, was it?
None of them is in the closet.

Yaxley

Last time here, I'd have been too small to walk,
When Freddie displayed his derelict retreat,
The Old School House (now renamed after him);
My grandmother, his devoted Tiggywinkle,
Benignly at ease in the big sloping fields.

And I can see why he'd have liked the place,
How the ancestral village touched his puritan soul;
While the vast airy spaces spoke of liberation,
His thatched hedgy corner offered sanctuary.
He craved, like all great artists, a modest nest.

Yet what am I doing, with notebook and camera,
Expecting the terror of dim recognition?
A trackless bridge, cow-parsley, distant traffic,
Cemented parish pump … but, beyond all this,
A scent on the air of the summer still to come.

After the Tempest

You know I always loathed the gang of them.
Two days at sea, already quarrelsome,
They squabble over titles, territory,
As if that mattered: their minds mutiny.
Meanwhile at last a kindly wind assists us;
The sky, as brittle-sharp as Venice glass,
Is cloudless; and the low late-autumn sun
Patterns the deck with shadow. An old man,
I sit here writing, unmissed, undisturbed
And (I confess) not wholly discontented:
My life's at last resolved, my long task ended,
As from the start I'd cunningly intended.
Strange, all the same, this interrupted cruise
To win back what I hadn't grieved to lose
And shan't know what to do with when we reach
The thriving port and populated beach:
An old world full of cares, affairs of state.
The point of islands is to isolate.

But there's my daughter: thinks she's royalty,
Looks forward to it, even may enjoy
A life of plots and power, of bugs and spies,
Grand gestures and expensive ceremonies.
I wish her well: or hope that food and wine
May recompense her for the asinine
Attentions of ambassadors and princes,

Bewigged buffoons and daisy-headed dunces.
Some have a taste for politics; but some
(Alas, such as myself) are overcome
By an urge to find in words the hint of meaning,
Whereas the courtly crew use them for preening –
The clause a comb, the phrase a powder-puff –
To prettify thin air, give form to fluff.

Of course, I could have stayed. You think so? No.
Not just because an end's ordained, although
It fell together like a perfect cadence,
But more because I'd outworn that pretence.
A man can't live surrounded by his errors:
I tried to civilise, to tame the terrors
Of things by nature nurtureless, untamed,
Where even sun and moon had been unnamed,
And every word rebounded as a curse,
As bad as courtly flummery, or worse!

There's no solution, then: maybe that's why,
Out here between dark sea and fading sky,
I feel this strange suspended happiness:
Things may go wrong, but things are more or less
For once beyond my meddlesome requests.
So, no more island shipwrecks, no more tempests.
When I get 'home', I'll treat the eye and ear,
Catch up with Caravaggio, and hear
What Monteverdi's written in my absence:
Who knows, perhaps there'll be a new Renaissance.
I've much to learn, and much more to forget
In my long autumn afternoon; and yet …

Before I lost my art, I saw the future:
How greed would feed on greed, and war on war;
Though man may learn to conquer pain, disease
Will deviously mutate. So death or madness
Must overtake the race, the failing planet.

And, worse, I came to see that this was right,
The globe's sole hope of greenness and rebirth,
Replenishing a grey, smoke-shrouded earth.
No states to govern, none to educate:
Do birds imagine? Butterflies create?
They are their art: have no need to invent
These foolish forms through which we represent
Our second-bestness. You of course will know
All this already, knew it long ago,
And yet … I almost said 'One last command',
Forgetting that I'd left you on our island.
The dusk draws on: I'm talking to the stars.
Perhaps, my absent friend, I always was.

Compost

in memory of Roy Fuller

The aged poet prods his compost heap,
Reminded of a former jest that he
Might make a decent mulch eventually,
For as you sow (he thinks) so shall you reap.
He wonders at the odd longevity
Not just of turnip, say, or cabbage-stalk,
But of hydrangea's mop-head levity.
A robin watches from his garden-fork,
With sly ironic glance, who seemingly
Approves and even shares the poet's mood,
Or humours him as harbinger of food.
The other thinks of how unerringly
All compost turns afresh, on its own terms,
To flower and fruit; to poets, robins, worms.

Poet and Cat

No doubt it's the subject of some aspiring PhD:
        If so, you'd better be
In there among the longer footnotes, Fishcat.
        Inimitable from that
Original head-through-window brisk self-introduction,
        You soon settled on
Our working relationship: I worked, you related;
        At least, you tolerated
First-draft furies from your chair near my desk, wheezing
        A bit, then sighing
With paws-over-ears resignation and a silly tabby grin.
        Some days, when I'd let you in,
A whole North Sea gale behind you, you'd land with the noise
        Of squashed teddy-bear toys;
Once mauled by a gull, scared of anything with wings,
        You'd chunter at starlings,
But happily tackle dogs, adults, over-attentive children;
        Rebuked too often
By a sniff and flick of the tail, I'd got your food fads known
        Better than my own.
Indestructible eccentric, how could you do this to me?
        Buried at sea:
Fit end for an Aldeburgh beach-cat, if end there had to be.

Hundred River

in memory of Adam Johnson

We came to Hundred River through a slow October,
      when earth is scented with everybody's past;
when late scabbed blackberries harden into devil's scars,
      untasted apples rot to bitter toffee.

Across reed-beds a track of blackened railway sleepers,
      a plank bridge lapped by barely-stirring water;
swans gargling silently in their fine indifference;
      above, a sky of urgent discursive geese.

Now the year has turned again and I am alone here,
      where willow-herb's dry white whiskers drift over
the brick-red spikes of sorrel and the gossiping reeds;
      and the river sullen, muddied after rain.

No movement in the woods but stealthy growth of fungus,
      hesitant leaf-drop, distant scuttle of deer:
In one marbled, stained oak-leaf I sense gigantic change,
      and in the drizzle feel the season fracture.

Celandines at Deanoak Brook

Some places stay for ever. Celandines
In bright rapacious grace beside the brook;
Mossed scent of earthy paths in bluebell woods;
Animal warmth of cloying straw-floored yards;
Deep meadows in their unwilled distances.

I'd play my game of hide-and-seek with life,
And win at every turn: they'd not catch me.
The garden-end and tunnelled undergrowth,
The roped and laddered oak – fine strategies
For a duke self-exiled from his childish court.

But hostile powers – Mynthurst, Stumblehole –
Defined themselves with cattle-grids or wires,
First iron curtains of the growing world:
The pebbled lane led on to tarmacked road,
Where bus-lamps shone in puddles after school.

Myself, I'd keep a life in walking distance,
Celandine-bright, mapped as a private planet.
In dreams, I'm in that other garden still:
Beyond the ditch, the fields remain unbounded,
But outer space begins at Norwood Hill.

Shell

I am schooled in the varieties of madness.
Feared beyond nickname, the Reverend dispensed
Lines for transcribing in copybook script,
Unflinching authority, Latin and caning,
As if his future depended upon it.

Borrowed on odd days, like the pitches,
With crinkle-cut hair and sandpapered face,
The games-master cultivated his own pleasures.
'Posture!' he'd yell: frozen already, we'd freeze.
On the way back to school, he'd de-bag stragglers.

After two years, we trekked upstairs to 'Shell':
A whiskery, tweedy, leathery sort of place
With squeaky hinged seats, a tuckshop cupboard,
An air of dim complicity. From Mr Salmond,
I learned only to evade his hand-picked attention.

There are photos to prove it. In one I'm slouched
Like a doll who's yet to have stuffing knocked in;
But later – I'm standing now, behind the Reverend –
There's that horrible confident smirk of survival:
I'd known most of the worst of the world by ten.

Old fools, the lot of them, not even doing
A quarter of their best, not caring or seeing
How much there was to give or how to give it;
Teaching instead bad habits by default –
Slow lessons in obsession, terror, guilt.

Road

for Nick Ash

Surely we've been here before. That road's
Strangely familiar, though the light has changed.
The echo's muted, like a song transposed.

That wayside scrub, in which so recently
Our hero planned his golden future, seems
Terminally autumnal, out of date;

And soon a pick-up truck or passing car
Will hungrily, rustily, splutter into shot,
Pass or pick up – it all depends – or not.

Above, beyond, a jagged high horizon
Shudders in haze: there's nothing much up there
But boulders, crags, sour scrags of vegetation,

A distant hint of empty winding track.
You know the line: 'This road will never end.'
Cue music. Roll end credits. Fade to black.

A Halfway House

Etched into dusk, it shows we're almost there:
Those lidded windows, biscuit-stucco walls
Between the water-meadows and the sea
Signal exact abandonment. Years drift:
Spring tides engulf it, lapping at the sills;
Gulls claim an apex among missing slates,
Shout their possession from the staring rafters;
Awash all winter, yet on summer nights
The beach will grow through shingle into sand
And turn this place inland.
                              A halfway life
May teach regard for this enduring ruin,
Weathered defender of uncertain ground,
And milestone marking that consoling point
Of nearing home, or starting out again.

IV
1998–2011

My Chelsea

My grandmother lived in a first-floor flat in Chelsea:
Limerston Street, a staid unfashionable bit.
She would not have thought of herself as exotic.

But I did, marvelling at her innocent grandeur,
Knowing that she would always be right,
As resonant and inclusive as her radiogram,

Despite odd finds among the ballet highlights:
Black-and-gold Crosbys or magenta Comos
Or, irresistible, Rose Murphy's 'Busy Line'.

Perhaps those were Auntie Cora's, whose name surely
Was that thing for getting middles out of apples
('Where's the Cora?' grumbled mother, rummaging).

But I digress as, inevitably, one does.
My Chelsea was a place at the end of journeys,
Green Southern to Victoria, then the 'inner' Circle –

I'd wonder what had happened to the outer one –
Which sometimes led to Ralph Lee's dental basement
With its buzzing, juddering insect-like black drill:

My mother's childhood dentist and then mine.
How could I guess that in my middle age
He'd gain, at 92, an MBE

For 'services to caravanning'? And sometimes
The journey led instead to Yeoman's Row,
To Freddie's, where my grandmother kept house,

Though what that meant I wasn't sure: only
Not to touch or explore, in spite of which
I'd tinkle on his sweet upright piano,

Until stilled by a gentle voice behind me.
'One day, my boy, you'll make a fine musician.'
I turned to find the choreographer

Smiling shyly. We never met again.
Our lives might intersect – in London, Suffolk –
Yet *in absentia*, the way they do,

Or don't. Perhaps my Chelsea was a place
In which a self might live another life,
The one in which the city didn't sour

Or country snare. We'd walk from Gloucester Road,
South Ken, Sloane Square, or take the 11 bus,
Arriving at a strange, familiar door

In a street that led to nowhere. 'What's down there?'
I wondered once. 'World's End,' my mother said.
World's *end*? My world had only just begun.

Across the Street

Across the street, their curtains are closed tight,
All day, all night, though people come and go:
A stubbly man who casts a cautious glance
Each way along the pavement; his plump wife
With boy or younger girl or blotchy dog –
Sometimes two of these, never all three.
Their door's always unlocked: they don't use keys.
And yet their house seems uninhabited:
Even that Friday night it gave a party,
All for itself, dancing to the foundations,
Or when slight shadows skim its glazed front door.

Across the street, they say: *Across the street,*
There's a man who keeps odd hours, who sits at home,
Hunched over a desk, or waves his arms about.
Odd parcels come by post; we've seen him too
Dashing to catch the five o'clock collection,
As if his so-called 'life' depended on it.
We think he drinks. His friends seem strange and few.

Across the street, I wonder if that's true.

1 August 2000

The purple buddleia has outreached itself;
Distended tendrils clog the narrow garden;
Drab blackbirds feed their damp prodigious young;
A wood pigeon calls the cows in after rain.

A quarter century! Its shrubs and birds
Growing, declining in the season's dance,
As I find, baffled by a long wet summer,
An unexpected break, another chance.

Results

Saturday teatime: football results slide by,
Unheeded, on the announcer's brylcreemed voice.

A lightship is moored close to the radio:
Its sails are twin clear bulbs in pallid shades.

Nil's neutral; three or four prompt mild surprise.
Teams fall like skittles: 'League Division Two …'

My father wants to know 'how Fulham got on';
I'm waiting for *Return to the Lost Planet*.

Meanwhile, I'll scan the KB's magic names,
Ranged in pennants on the glowing wavebands:

Green, amber, red, three slim inverted signals.
I light on Allouis, Kalundbourg, Motala:

Are they cities, with castles, dukes and princes,
Or tall lost masts out there in the humming dusk?

Thanks

I.O.J.P. 1911–1994

And you thought I'd forgotten. Hardly. It's just
that the book's last poem had to be for you,
made of these stammering, rueful syllabics,
the closest thing that poets have to silence.
Though in truth I shan't forget our silences:
yours, as I thought, fraught with disdain and distance,
mine full of priggish intellectual anger –
a line of communication, after all,
since in the end we knew each other too well
to need to speak.
     Outside, slow November dusk:
this is the moment we depressives like best,
when jabbering daylight no longer nags at us
and melancholia makes us feel at home;
time to close curtains, get the tea, look forward
to sherry, supper and a long safe evening;
then crossword, concert on the Third, a nightcap,
and who's to worry if we should fall asleep?
Knowing this, one might be inclined to wonder
how you put up with the years in the City,
the office, the trains, the European trips
to glass factories where they never rumbled
your consummate disguise. But I did. Even
on holiday, you'd do your best, as homesick
as Mr Woodhouse.
     Like me, you loathed summer:
ill at ease on beaches, though fond of cricket.
Saturday mornings, whatever the season,
you came into your own – the sort of father
every boy wants, and somehow all the better
for being that special weekend creation:
we were let loose, while mother shopped in Reigate,
on our equal, comradely exploration –

Finch's cycle shop; or, up a steep alley,
beyond the Town Hall, La Trobe's model railways;
Forte's ice-cream at Mrs Lee's in Bell Street;
and doughnuts to take home for elevenses.
Yes, you indulged me, by indulging yourself:
were seldom, I now think, happier.
                                        Of course,
it couldn't last: that's childhood for you. Going
away to school, I lost you: it had to be,
for the son whom you wanted to have everything
you'd lacked in your education couldn't be
the son who'd follow you into the business,
who was also the son you wanted; besides,
that barely imagined public school turned out
to be one where masters read the *Guardian*
and talked about Sartre. Soon I'd be writing home
to declare myself an 'interlectual':
you simply corrected the spelling, as when
'This is a wasted stamp, this a waisted stamp',
followed by one stuck uselessly on the page
and another with neat cuts to its middle,
put me right on that score.
                                   I kept on learning
from you longer than you guessed: as a student
in the silly, permissive nineteen-sixties –
literary, leftish, decidedly queer –
I'd still wear jacket and tie to seminars,
in tepid debates invoke Uncle Enoch,
kinship his Brummie vowels made unlikely,
though sure to fire the rebels of '68!
(What's worse, or better, I surmised even then
that one reason they couldn't stomach Powell
was his wry assumption that they'd read Virgil.)
You admired his intransigent honesty –
and, yes, so did I, shameless contrarian,
my father's son.
                      Contrarians don't get on,

unless they negotiate a steady truce,
which we didn't. Should we have done? I doubt it.
Awkwardly different yet exactly alike
was how we were planned to be, if there's a plan,
yet there were times when each might have intervened:
I should have urged you to take more exercise,
and you should have talked me out of starting that
ridiculous bookshop. There'd have been no point:
when either of us knew we were being daft,
we'd only grow more obstinate.
                                              Still, I don't know
whether you ever reached where you were going;
whether at last in Orford you were happy;
whether you were proud – or not ashamed – of me.
'You can't do better than your best' you'd tell me,
but so often I've not done that. It's dark now,
freezing hard outside, another winter's night,
as I write these lines: they're not the half of it.
If reading is what completes a poem, then
of course this poem can never be complete:
all it can edge or stumble towards is what,
holding your hand for the first time since childhood,
at that June lunchtime in a hospital room,
I tried to whisper but you quite understood.
Thanks. And that indeed is what I meant to say.

Three Sightings of W.G. Sebald

1

In the Jolly Sailor, you prod at skate and chips,
Having just been ferried back from 'the island' –
Now visitable though not demystified.
There's strange abandonedness at Shingle Street,
But nowhere hugs its secrecy like this.
You look weary. Skate's a difficult fish.

2

In the Jubilee Hall, you read from *The Rings of Saturn*
As if you'd written it in English; are coy
About translators. The first questioner wants to know
Why the pages of his copy have come loose.
Tonight, a Brendel concert at the Maltings:
These twinkling Germanic melancholics!

3

In the darkest corner of a Bungay junkshop,
You carefully leaf through the sepia postcards
As if they tell your story: which they do.
These images meld into narrative;
The narrative enacts your images.
Mind-traveller, time-traveller, you are the alchemist.

Covehithe

In my dream they said: 'You must go to Covehithe.'
I crossed over the causeway between two blue lakes
And I found myself on a long forest path
With a few wooden shacks and a glimpse of the sea.
I thought after all it was a place that might suit me.
But they said: 'You must learn from your mistakes.'

So, I have come to Covehithe. Low winter sun
Scans fields of pigs, dead skeletal trees,
Collapsing cliffs. There are ships on the horizon.
The great church, wrecked by Civil War, not storm,
Now shields a smaller church from further harm.
And they were wrong: I like it as it is.

Two Adolescents

They remind me, with their sloping shrugging gait,
Slack confidential chat, taking the dog
For its evening walk, these two, they remind me

Of warm September nights when we talked and talked
Until dawn brought us sleep. They remind me
Of the times I used to tell you everything.

The Picture of the Mind

for Peter Scupham

He meant of course 'the picture in the mind' –
Those images of origins and ends
That danced into a world he'd left behind –
But what's a preposition between friends?

'I cannot paint,' he said, 'what then I was';
And then he painted it. A nice conceit?
Or did the words seem vulnerable because
Such part-disclosure must be indiscreet?

If so, his indiscretions served him well:
For half-disclosing is what poems do,
In hints and emblems seeming to reveal
The picture of the mind – iambic, true.

Reading Proust on Aldeburgh Beach

How near to us they are, these distant children
Whose voices scatter shingle, glance off walls,
Returning. 'You can come in ours, if you like,'
One shouts, pointing at a boat which is not his.

And how such games of vacant possession
Will linger to haunt their deals and their dreams,
In the grey blur of morning, or the fertile dark,
Or the patchwork shadows of late afternoon.

The past, it seems, is not a foreign country,
Nor even down the road in the next town:
It is here and now, at the edge of England,
In children's voices and the arc of a gleam,

Where sunlight and sealight join in the dance
Of images we choose to call remembrance.

Waveney

for Robert Wells

1. *Ditchingham Dam*

It takes days after rain for the water to rise:
False calm, a fatal illness in remission,
Comforts the sunlit fields. The river sulks;
Then, grumbling, slowly starts to rouse itself;
Barges about, flings upstream vegetation
On tangled banks; and fills to teacup-brim,
Tea-coloured, stirred. Its weather is historic.

And now the meadows soak and bloat like sponges,
Their surface stippled with the tips of grass:
Cattle crowd strange islands; ducks and swans
Find new amazing lakes; across the fields,
The bypass has become a distant shore.
Along the dam, life puts up barricades,
Safe beyond each shut and sandbagged door.

2. The Metfield Imp

He is a tutivillus or a titivil:
His task, to gather up into his sack
Mistakes and mangled words, which he conveys
And scatters on his travels underground.
Thus, if the road to Hell (as Johnson said)
Is paved with good intentions, then this imp
Supplies the paving-slabs: might that explain
His lolling tongue and wide salacious grin?

Perhaps: though if we guessed our errors' value,
Translated into paths for fallen souls,
Would not such faults be easier to assuage?
The imp looks unconvinced: he's heard it all.
Meanwhile, beneath the tower the Metfield Clock,
A broken heart, ticks gravely in its cage.

3. The Minster

The past gets lost: we search, research for it
In secret places. Here, at the hidden heart
Of a sacred country, may be where to start,

Or where to end. Still almost out of reach,
Still glossy-guidebook-proof and tourist-free,
Hawthorn and oak and freshly planted beech

Surround a shadowed clearing and these stones –
A little church for Bishop Herbert, really –
Now bedded down in nettles, celandines.

Thatched, round-ended, with a tall square tower
Is how the artist sees it, yet the Minster
Was disused by the fourteenth century: its power

Lies in that vanishing, that ever-growing
Vacancy. Our knowledge is unknowing.

4. *Jane's Island*

It reconfigures childhood myths: not Circe,
But *Swallows and Amazons*, *The Wind in the Willows*.
Across a wobbly bridge, this private island
Is where bulbs prosper and ducklings are saved
From becoming carp's breakfasts. A legislature
Unknown to the quotidian world obtains here:
Benign despotism of conservationist, gardener,
Reminds us that 'privilege' means 'private law'.

And a river island seems right for a novelist,
Whose universe is almost like our own,
Though more portably confined. No such luck
For the unterritorial poet; he, ugliest duckling,
Must be tipped off the bank to fend for himself,
Downstream to the staithe and the critical carp.

5. *Across the Bridge*

I once knew a man who was so Suffolk he
Couldn't abide this view across the Waveney:
The sight of Norfolk more than he could stand.
He'd not have been amused to learn I found
In him a match for Joseph Calloway:
That character in Greene's *Across the Bridge*,
Another fraught observer at the edge,
Marooned in Mexico, watching the USA.

Up a lazy river, though not quite the kind
Hoagy Carmichael must have had in mind.
All's lazy here: all residues drift down
This winding street from a sour, shabby town,
Clog at the bridge. Yes, I once knew and know
A man who can't abide this. Time to go.

For Andrew Mackinlay Esq, MP

on the death of Dr David Kelly

He was, of course, a sacrifice, and *chaff*'s perhaps the word for it;
But chaff's a noble thing to be, beside this heap of shit.

At the End of the Line

At the end of the line, there are ships nudging the quay.
There is water bluer than you might have imagined.

Commercial Road's terraces should gleam with colours
Borrowed from harbour lights: it could be Copenhagen.

Except, at the end of the line, the station windows are boarded.
The last train has gone. There are people shuffling in gutters.

Brave nautical statues shade their eyes against wasteland:
Tarnished Carr of the Ocean looks baffled by 'Cash 4 U'.

And the smell of a fried past wafts over the swing bridge
With its unblinking message: *When red man shows wait HERE.*

And yes, at the end of the line, I am always waiting.
I am always waiting for you at the end of the line.

Dusk in the Surrey Hills

Such sly transitions, where lane shades into track,
and track into path, are things that I should know;
like a trick of the light, or a change of key,
or a shift from iambic to syllabic.

And I do know them: here the path limps uphill,
past a dense hedge, a dim mysterious lodge,
and a low field in which a dog stands howling,
while another looks dispassionately on;

two tails wag, and they resume their devotions,
confirming my grateful insignificance;
a rabbit pops up to peer at me; and three
hurrying muntjacs crash past without a glance.

There is pungency in the old rot of yews,
of a past well stewed: its aromatic fug
jostles teasingly with lighter, sharper beech:
a single sniff tells me this is Colley Hill.

Suddenly I'm lost: lostness swoops down like night,
and I realise that what I have mislaid
is not so much the path as the sure instinct
which once would have got me home. Another dog,

this time made of brownish carpet, scuttles by,
taking a dog-sized short-cut no good to me;
and yet, at the next step, my feet find their way,
report back via some forgotten sensory

circuit that these log-faced muddy steps will lead
round a beech-choked crater, and then down again,
where a kind of rustic timbered balustrade
should prevent even the confused from falling.

Strange how panic subsides to knowledge; stranger,
coming from yew-shadow to the last of light
on the path between the fields above The Clears,
to see carpet-dog and owner further on,

in confident possession of their landscape,
striding downhill, where ghostly Shetland ponies
nuzzle the barbed-wire fence, expecting windfalls
from the garden opposite, which once was home.

The Nature of Things

for Rod Shand

Polonius: *What do you read, my lord?*
Hamlet: *Words, words, words.*
                    Hamlet, II, 2, 191–2

Apple

An apple on a leafless branch in autumn holds the winter back;
And here, an Apple on the desk, my fruitful glowing Mac.

Books

Books are good to have around:
They decorate an empty space,
Lend graceless rooms a borrowed grace;
In noisy homes they deaden sound.

With what absurd self-consciousness
We handle them: the more we know,

The less we sense the way to show
Intuitive receptiveness.

The bibliophile's or scholar's need
To index, date, or cross-refer
Is always there to interfere
With what we once had: a good read.

Carcanet

*Car*canet? Car*can*et? Who could know
What it meant, how to pronounce the thing?
And who'd have guessed, those thirty years ago,
How many pearls would gather on its string?

Doves

Two collared doves feeding, their clockwork nods
    Discreetly out of synch:
One pecks demurely at a crust of bread,
    The other stops to drink,
As peaceable as legend decrees,
    Or so I choose to think.

Epigrams

Of epigrams (and epigraphs) beware:
They smile most charmingly before they snare.
Regard them as a double-sided cloak:
The sweetest grin conceals the sourest joke.

Of epigrams (not epigraphs) take heed:
Be sure that what you see is what you read;
For what you see may dance before your eyes,
But what you read will leave you old and wise.

Fog

Auden thanked you: now the thanks decay.
Gershwin too; though Billie Holiday
Transformed her foggy day in London town:
The sun (she sang) was shining upside-down.

Garden

My garden is bounded by an ancient wall,
Watched over by two towers, round Trinity
And square St Mary's, whose proximity
Informs its habits: knotty shrubs grow tall
And climbers grasp towards the crowded sky.

Hands

Scabbed and scratched by cooking, gardening,
And middle age's dim incompetence,
You have claimed unlooked-for independence.
You have become recalcitrant. You drop things.

And yet, hands, your skills are undiminished
Where most they matter. You manage a signature,
Most days, and can tackle an easy sonata.
You tie impenetrable knots. You are good in bed.

Ice

O for a muse of fire, or even ice,
Which would (as Robert Frost observed) suffice.

Jazz

Not blue. Deep green of Bechet's sad soprano;
Rich terracotta red of Satchmo's horn;
Steely violet glow of Parker's alto;
Ochres and sepias of Duke Ellington ...

An old unfathomable love: now that's blue.

Key

That key he gave me years ago
Slept in a drawer, cocooned with dust;
Its blunted teeth were stained with rust.
Its function I no longer knew.

Yet, far away, a slow clock ticks
And patient time comes circling back.
The sun turns through its zodiac.
The minutes pass. The lock unsticks.

Light

Light falls in its haphazard way,
Illuminates the here and there,
Enhances space, transfigures air.
It blunders in where shadows play.

The stunts it pulls as clouds roll by
Must always take us by surprise,
As scenes catch light before our eyes:
A Constable sea; a Turner sky.

Music

No, Pater, no:
All art does not aspire to its condition.
Haydn, Mozart, Schubert, Mahler, Britten
Speak what we cannot speak, beyond the sayable,
Translate the universe into the playable.
Our lesser arts must learn how to be humble.
And words? Just listen to them stumble.

Name

My name and I are not on speaking terms.
It owns an overdraft, a little fame,
A modest house, a car; yet all confirms
One sombre fact: I do not love my name.

And yet, why should I? That's for others, surely:
No earthly point becoming covetous
About a thing so near, so arbitrary!
Just watch yourself, as Zeus said to Narcissus.

Oaks

Bronze oaks stretch out against November sky.
They have sculpted their own trunks. They rule the fields:
They make the gangling pylons insecure.

I'd leave my bike near here and catch a lift
To school. Returning in the afternoon,
I'd often find the saddle acorn-strewn.

Those acorns, some of them, must be fine trees
By now, though merely twigs compared with these.

Irons Bottom, Surrey

Prayer

Prayer came to me one autumn night
    In frosty Warwickshire:
I sought for words against the dark,
        Though whether God would hear

I hardly cared or guessed. That was
        Some half a life ago:
The habit formed, it captured me
        In its warm mist, and so

When I repeat the form of words,
        I God or self deceive,
For I have never ceased to pray
        Nor started to believe.

Quires

And yet, what is belief? I think of Sundays
When, long ago, we'd make the chancel ring
With our transfigured voices, and shall always
Be drawn to 'Quires and Places where they sing'.

Roads

Roads are linear, and so
You might expect them to be straight;
Yet roads both twist and deviate –
The back and forth, the high and low –

And seem perversely to avoid
The places signposts advertise,
Beguilingly, on either side.
Those villages that roads despise

Remain unvisited, unknown,
Unspoilt perhaps; for who can tell
Who travels, sadly and alone,
The tarmac lines from hell to hell?

Squib

A squib, you see, is what this is:
Too damp to spark, or even fizz.

Tracks

Tracks seen from the window of a moving train
Run with us brightly in parallel, then gradually
Fade, like old friends, from view. We glimpse them again,
Among nettles and willow-herb, neglected now and rusty,
Breaking under the strain of keeping up with us,
Until they reach their broken buffers, we our terminus.

Umbrage

I'd like to think that Umbrage
Is a posher sort of Uxbridge:
A spa wrapped in the Sussex Downs,
One letter south from other towns
Like Tunbridge Wells or Tonbridge,

Which ladies from Jane Austen
Could decorously get lost in.
To sip at its medicinal spring
Would prove the cure for anything:
They'd call it 'Taking Umbrage'.

Vanity

Ah, vanity: I remember
Posting off my masterpiece,
As an ambitious teenager,
To a firm in Southend on Sea
Which advertised in *Private Eye*.

I was the great discovery
Whom they'd be proud to publish,
If I'd just send them fifty quid.
I thought it better spent on drink.
A lesson learnt, I think.

Wheels

Wheels are circular, and so
You might expect them to repeat
Some self-perpetuating feat;
But wheels engage with what's below.

Thus, unless a rocking pram
Should choreograph their static dance,
Wheels meet at each circumference
Newly charted tarmacadam.

The fascination of what's found
Meshes with known patterns turning,
Held at the hub, forever singing
The same song over different ground.

X

Skiving off rugby
One bleak afternoon,
I sneaked into the matinée
X at the Odeon.

In the side corridor,
I switched my school tie
Before reaching the foyer.
They took my money.

Just as it should be.

Youth

'And in my youth …' 'Which youth is that?' you'll say,
'The one I saw you with the other day?'

Zero

What a bunch of no-hopers these tail-enders are
For anyone seeking an icon or hero:
There's whimsical Zeus, but elsewhere the score
Is sadly, emphatically, zilch, even zero.

Route 424

We'd catch the 424 from Reigate Station –
Peter, Nigel and I – as if we owned the bus:
First on, grabbing the long back seat upstairs.

We'd made our way through privet-hedged suburbia –
All yappy dogs and frosted-glass front-doors
And signs that said *No Hawkers, No Circulars* –

Across a shrub-mazed roundabout and under
The railway bridge adorned with bad attempts
At genital representation and with comments

Unflattering to our despised headmaster,
Then loitered at the shop in Holmesdale Road
Where, like a mad chemist, white-aproned Mr Dodd

Made brightly coloured test-tube-shaped iced lollies,
Entirely flavourless, but costing a mere penny.
Thus strangely fortified, we'd think ourselves ready

To catch the 424 from Reigate Station,
Rattling down to the Red Cross, High Street, Bell Street
(Where sundry lesser mortals climbed aboard)

Before heaving over Cockshot Hill to Woodhatch:
Nigel lived there, beyond a service road,
In the kind of house you'd only build from Bayko –

Thirties, bay-windowed, with a mirror-twin
In an interminable parade of pairs of twins.
I pitied him but, even then, kept quiet about it.

Peter, by contrast, lived at Sidlow Bridge
And by magic could command the bus to stop
Opposite his house. He was a sly child

With a mouth like a letterbox, scheming eyes,
And I admired him hugely: what's more, his house
Stood on its own, with outbuildings and grounds.

I fancied myself as an apprentice crim,
Certain that if there was no good to be up to,
Peter would know of it, take me along with him –

Though if he did I have, of course, forgotten.
More likely those were thoughts that lingered in
The darkening upper deck once he'd got off:

As he crossed the road, walked up the drive, I'd look
Over my shoulder – the first friend I'd met
Who seemed to be worth watching out of sight.

And then I'd be alone, dim egg-cupped bulbs
In the curved cream ceiling holding off the dusk,
As lights came on in dolls' house living-rooms,

Where boys like me took off their coats and caps
Or flung down satchels, ravenous for tea.
Now houses gave way to open fields and copses

Until we reached my stop at Irons Bottom;
I'd fetch my bike from Freddy Laker's yard
And ride down Deanoak Lane, the last mile home.

The Garden at Clears

'It is closing time in the gardens of the West.'
Cyril Connolly

1

A shingled single track; a broken gate,
Unhinged and folded back against the hedge;
A late spring day in 1958 …
Time hovers like a syrphid at the edge

Of some gigantic leaf: slow minutes pass
As gravel shifts and settles in the lane.
A spider weaves its way among the grass.
The sun is veiled by clouds and clears again.

At length two boys on bicycles arrive
(One is my friend John, the other's me),
Who shade their eyes and squint along the drive:
Two children seeing what there is to see.

But what is there to see? A gate, a track,
Between two grassy fields, a flowering cherry
Disconsolate in blossom's aftershock,
Its fallen petals scattered like confetti;

A wonky board, 'For Sale'. The agent's name
Is Gascoigne-Pees: 'Of course he does,' I say.
Now what, a thought ago, had been a game
Acquires the shaping hint of destiny:

The rutted track becomes a path between
Two sloping lawns, untended and unmown;
A landscaped garden shading into green,
Its rockeries and parterres overgrown;

A neat white building locked into the hill.
No one at home: there hasn't been for years.
The house waits in its leafy pellicle
For somebody to reinhabit Clears.

This isn't us, not quite. But John has found
One unlatched window where the upper floor
Comes up against the steeply rising ground,
An open invitation to explore:

And so, my friend and I, we amble through
Rooms where the dusty light of afternoon
Glows on the present's ghostly residue,
Glints at the future. I shall live here soon.

2

One warm August day, we picnicked in the big back shed,
Among the random objects that had yet to find their homes
In still unfurnished rooms.
What had they taken on, what in the world had possessed them,
My parents, to buy this weird house wedged into a hillside
With its untameable acres of landscaped wilderness?
(Later they'd say their ten-year-old son had persuaded them.)
Eating our sandwiches among mangles and mowers,
We felt like the Borrowers:
A giant cotton-reel for a table wouldn't have seemed out of place.

That was the best year, '58–'59,
When I biked to St Mary's, came home for lunch,
A time when lessons were vexatious interruptions
To my life of cycling, roaming the Surrey Hills
Or exploring the garden at Clears.
I'd commandeered that big back shed and filled it
With a wind-up gramophone, an ancient typewriter,
And junk purloined from old George Wickens' yard

In Nutley Lane (the Borrowers again).
One day I'd turn up with a box of rare 78s,
The next with a brown rabbit in my saddlebag.

The garden shook off its green surprise and flourished,
Prodigious with bulbs in spring – a drift of snowdrops
Cushioning the dell – and with autumn fruits.
Up a ladder, surrounded by a crowd of feasting wasps,
I picked Tsar plums (there were enough to go round),
Or learned to grasp Blenheims from the highest branches
With a long-handled apple-picker.
The fig trees flapped their elephantine leaves
In fruitless gestures;
Rhubarb stretched out its raw enormous limbs;
Rampant asparagus spread like a dithery, feather-headed weed;
The cute bamboo had grown to an impenetrable copse,
Watched over by a stately copper beech
While, ranged at the end of the lower terraced lawn,
Our landmark team of eleven Lombardy poplars
Stood to ragged attention – with one stump for referee.
How could this ever end? But I went away to school,
Became a boy with a divided soul.

On Boxing Day in '62 it snowed;
It snowed all through the cold new year to Easter.
We put chains on the Wolseley to get along the track
To Colley Lane; the bicycle was useless.
I trekked up to the hills in my huge boots,
Snowballing the friskily silly dog,
The cat in obstinate pursuit, paw-prints chin-deep,
The Shetland ponies more stumpy-legged than ever,
Creamy-brown sheep lined up on the white horizon.
At school, the playing-field and park were lost in drifts –
We ran on silent, frozen roads –
But when the holidays arrived it was still there, the garden,
Pallid after its long cold storage.

It was the year I discovered modern jazz, Stravinsky;
Read Thom Gunn, Iris Murdoch; started to write …
One evening I cycled to the Odeon in Redhill
To see *The Servant*: I was fifteen,
Hungry for experience and bad company,
Gratefully accosted by a man twice my age.
When I got home, my mother, anxious on the landing,
Was waiting up for me: had I enjoyed the film?
Perhaps I'd better not discuss it with my father
Who 'wouldn't really like that sort of thing'.
So many doors closed with the bedroom door;
Then I lay awake, listening to trains in the valley,
A nearby owl and the great immeasurable dark –
Alienated, empowered, and free.
The garden at Clears was growing away from me.

3

All's fallen into autumn, all's at rest:
The burdened apple-tree, the tangled vine.
It is closing time in the gardens of the West.

Leaves settle slowly into mulch, compressed
As trodden grapes to concentrated wine:
All's fallen into autumn, all's at rest.

We drank the noble vintages, the best;
Now others trickle out their slow decline:
It is closing time in the gardens of the West.

The bird returns to its abandoned nest,
These tattered remnants of a grand design:
All's fallen into autumn, all's at rest,

And dark horizons prove the stormiest.
Thus Connolly in 1949:
'It is closing time in the gardens of the West.'

The written page reverts to palimpsest;
The ink runs white; the letters disentwine.
All's fallen into autumn, all's at rest,
It is closing time in the gardens of the West.

Adam

Be with me, quiet ghost, as the short days lengthen,
As blackthorn winter staggers into spring:
Where my resolves are weakest, you will strengthen.

Be with me, quiet ghost, as the long days shorten,
And light begins its slow unravelling:
Where my resolves are slackest, you will tauten.

My friend, my reader, you are still nearby,
Your wry wise presence undiminishing:
Be with me, quiet ghost, as the seasons die.

Finzi's Orchard

There is special power in an adoptive landscape,
Unsmudged by ties of birth or ancestry,
Unburnished by false childhood memory.

Hampshire downland: Church Farm, Ashmansworth.
'This,' he said, 'is what I have always longed for.'
Not meaning, I think, anything as easy

As an edenic ideal, but rather the place
To do what he did best: to cultivate
Rare apple trees, collect rare poets, write

An English music – more than English because
His outsider's eye and ear have given it
Such frail disenchantment, such haunted repose.

Shakespeare, Milton, Traherne, Wordsworth, Hardy;
Their words are kerned, finding new edges,
New spaces between them, and new purity

Of diction. There is fresh wind in the trees;
A russet windfall nestles in the grass;
The russet clarinet rests on its bed of strings.

Was and Is

I was the child who scarred his forehead
Riding his tricycle past an open window;
Who lied to doctors, dentists and opticians;
Whose feet defeated even Daniel Neal.

I was the child who fainted in assembly;
Who ran cross-country to be on my own;
Whose mind slid past classroom windows
To alight on tombstones, junkshops, sky.

I was the child who made a world in a shed;
Who talked to animals, birds and sunsets;
Who built an igloo from the first snowfall.
I am the man who is almost none the wiser.

The Boy on the Bus

I am the boy on the bus. Soft milky light
Is gently bathing frantic city streets;
Somewhere a cheerful urban bird is singing.
It's good up here. Things may turn out all right.

I am the boy on the bus. And yet elsewhere,
My friends are now unsafely underground –
As I should be, aboard the Northern Line.
There is no choice: I have to join them there.

I am the boy on the bus. I don't know how
The twists of destiny have brought me here.
I am the boy on the bus. We've turned a corner.
I only know I have to do this now.

July 2005

Point-to-Point

in memory of Bill Richardson

Heathfield it was, Dickie Severn and the rest,
Campers and champers on Easter Monday,
Rollers and Land Rovers, ludicrous picnics;
Losing bets on horses, too, of course.
And the booze! Sandy, red-faced, in his element,
Impervious to us, the ironic young,
Stifling our delight at the silliness of it all.

That's forty years ago: more, probably.
And when, a decade later, I caught sight of you,
Owlishly tight in the White Hart one night
Among the gas lamps and the invasive vines,
I knew that I knew you from somewhere else,
A former life, and what's more you knew me.

Less simple than it sounds, this sort of knowing:
Your mind (and why you bludgeoned it) acute
Beyond what's bearable. Examples? Certainly.
Scroll on another ten to a windy spring,
Aldeburgh again, my annual writing visit,
Yet different this time: I'd not meant to be alone.
You saw that at once, although I'd never said.
'Boyfriend stood you up?' you asked. 'Thought so.'
(Which, Adam, was why you had to come next year.)

Scroll on again to when you met my mother:
Your courtesy impeccable, always 'Mrs Powell'.
Now you seemed like a prep-school headmaster
Or stooping clergyman, knowing yet remote:
'Charming lady,' you said, 'but unimaginative.'
And yes, it had baffled me all my life, her lack
Of interest in what went on in others' heads,
Including (I need hardly add) my own.

Inseparable, of course, from those terrible dogs:
That's you with the whippet on *A Halfway House*,
Battling your way along Crag Path into the mist,
Guy's painting so much more evocative than this.
Drunk in David's Place, alarm-clock in your pocket,
Dog on a dressing-gown cord, while the old rascal
Poured after-hours Scotch by his pencil-torchlight:
Never quite my thing, though I saw that for you
It recalled fifties Soho, at Muriel's, or Mabel's.
You'd history there – I remember Stephen Spender
Cutting you dead over some unhealed old wound –
From the days when you'd been a promising poet.

Tunbridge Wells, absurdly, was your family home
Until that Christmas and the terrible accident
At Snape crossroads, in which your brother died.
You came to Suffolk then and never went back.
It's no distance from here to there: a couple of hours
Will do it on a good day, yet I know it seemed
Another world. Seems so still: that immense
Gradually unravelling distance to the finishing line.

Me and Mr Jones

One side of Church Street was a bombed crater,
Fenced off with wonky posts and wire netting,
Torn and distorted like an old string vest:
We'd chuck pebbles from the school crocodile.

Across the street, where the Old Wheel teashop
Tottered genteelly, an anonymous parade:
Outfitter, off-licence, grocer, estate agent,
And RHYTHM, that strange unspellable word.

I'd park my bike against the double-stepped kerb
Outside the record shop. The manager, Mr Jones,
Crinkly-haired and smelling of the wardrobe,
Greeted me like an old friend. I was ten years old.

Did he guess at his corrupting influence?
I think he simply saw a fellow addict
To pamper with free catalogues and supplements,
Spare cardboard sleeves or bargain-price deletions.

Most of what I'd buy was junkshop stuff,
Threepence or sixpence, but sometimes I'd save up
Until I had the astonishing six bob
To become a paying customer of Mr Jones.

The little pegboard-walled audition room:
Last year's top twenties dangling from a pin,
Frayed posters for forgotten pantomimes,
Giant portraits – Mantovani, Vera Lynn –

Caught on the cusp of the almost obsolete;
The steady electric hum, emphatic click
Of sapphire to shellac as the pick-up dropped
On the latest by Elvis or the Everlys.

Then the purchase made, the record wrapped
In its red-and-white striped bag proclaiming
There is no form of music without Rhythm,
Lovingly nursed through its two-wheeled journey,

Hugged to my shed at the bottom of the garden,
Played there to a captive audience of ants
(A bright new needle in my wind-up HMV),
Catalogued and shelved. I see a habit,

Lifelong, clearly forming. More than that:
The fragile thing, brought safely home to cherish,
Had a sort of sacred magic which would vanish
When discs were vinyl, gramophones plugged in.

Shutting Down

'We've moved her,' they say, 'to a single room.
We thought she would be more comfortable.'
I read their faces to decode what this means:
Her condition would distress the other patients.

Driving in, this placid summer evening,
I prayed: let it be one thing or the other,
A proper recovery or a rapid end,
Anything but unwilling, lingering half-life.

She no longer tries to speak as I hold her hand,
Until shaken by a cough trapped in her throat.
I run for help, but the words 'death rattle' check me.
'She just decided,' says the sister, 'to shut down.'

The Journal of Lily Lloyd

in memory of Dulcie Powell, née Lloyd (1922–2008)

1

The last day of October 1919:
Waterloo Station: not feeling excited,
sort of feeling all upside-down. Quite a crowd
to see us off. In the train to Southampton,
a dear little Scotch boy who'd been to visit
his granny in Scotland and was very pleased
to be going back to the sunshine, saying
such funny native words. We reached Southampton
about 12.30: there was the lovely boat,
the *Balmoral Castle*. What a huge vessel!
There were thirty young married couples on board,
all English girls trying their luck in S.A.
I learnt that I was in a two-berth cabin
with a nice young woman called Mrs Ritchie.
Lunch was laid in the big dining saloon,
the stewards all looking very clean and fresh
in their little white jackets: a lovely lunch,
plenty of everything, huge dishes of fruit.
We were leaning over the side of the boat,
as they were drawing up the landing-bridges,
when a man came alongside taking photos:
he said if I'd throw down a penny ha'penny
he'd send one to my home address in London.

Inserted here, a sepia photograph:
'R.M.S. Balmoral Castle'. There they are:
Lily, in her crumpled fur-trimmed coat and hat
decorated as if with fancy icing,
beams with ingenuous goodness; meanwhile Jack,
in military cap and greatcoat, smiles wryly,
with deep-set eyes, broad nose and semaphore ears.
He looks like me. We meet, after ninety years.

The ropes were being hauled in and the engines
bumping, a dockside band struck up 'Good Byee',
and at last we were moving, oh so slowly;
then the band had changed its tune to 'Auld Lang Syne',
and as you looked along the line of young girls,
all had tears in their eyes. We couldn't help it:
not one of us knew what was in store for us.
Soon we were going full steam ahead, along
the English Channel, and it was almost dark.

What a head I had when I woke next morning!
I felt I couldn't lift it off the pillow.
The stewardess brought cups of tea: awful stuff,
stewed, coloured with what tasted like Ideal Milk,
and with so much sugar we couldn't drink it.
It made Mrs Ritchie sick. Just after that,
her husband came, helped her dress and get on deck.
After a struggle, I dressed and crawled on deck,
staggered to the rail and was terribly ill.
I looked round for Jack but he wasn't up yet:
he wasn't attentive like Mr Ritchie.
The pair of us stayed in this horrible state
until we reached the island of Madeira.

We first saw it looking like a huge black cloud
standing on the water; as we drew nearer,
we could see the hollows in the hills, and trees,
and red, green, blue and white roof tops of houses.
As soon as we anchored in Funchal Harbour,
hundreds of tugs and rowing-boats came to us;
natives clambered up the side of the vessel
like a lot of monkeys, with their wares to sell,
chairs, tables, baskets, hand embroidery work.
There were lots of naked little boys swimming,
shouting to the passengers 'Penny I dive',
diving like fish to get the coins thrown to them.

We were off again: all was merry and bright,
and everyone was well over seasickness.
There were all sorts of games and competitions,
impromptu dances and a fancy dress ball,
a big boxing tournament, and the Three Scamps,
the music hall artistes, gave us several turns.
Monday 16th of November, at 5 a.m.,
we arrived in Cape Town and were woken by
everybody's husband shouting, 'Come and look
at God's own country!' We dressed and went on deck.
A glorious sight it was: Table Mountain
and Lion's Head towering over the docks,
lovely blue sky and not a cloud to be seen.

2

Myself and two other girls were left on board
while our husbands were taken to Maitland Camp
to get their discharge. But then, when Jack came back,
I understood the lies he'd been telling me:
he had deceived us all. He said I must go
at once to the Governor General Fund,
ask for two nights' shelter in Cape Town, rail fares
to Johannesburg and a week's shelter there.
I swear I would never have got off that boat
if it had been leaving again straight away.
But I put my pride in my pocket and went:
I had made my bed and I must lie on it,
and hope for better luck in the Transvaal.

The man at the Governor General Fund
took my hand: 'Do you mean to say you've married
an apprentice fitter and come all this way?
I admire your pluck.' We got our two days' board
at Small's Hotel: a bedroom overlooking
Devil's Peak. That evening, after dinner,

we went round Table Mountain in a tramcar,
arum lilies growing wild along the side;
we also bought some silver leaves from a man,
as we didn't go high enough to pick them.
(Here, four glued-in dried leaves 'off Table Mountain'.)
Next day, we went to Muizenberg – it was there
that I first saw people riding on surfboards –
then to a pretty suburb, Clifton-on-Sea:
Jack was one of those 'live for today' people,
so we decided to make the most of it.

Next morning at ten o'clock we caught the train
to Johannesburg. Those trains are great big things:
each carriage holds six passengers; there are bunks
to let down for sleeping, washbasin, mirror,
card table, even a little balcony
with tip-up seats if you want a breath of air.
It was all lovely and green until we reached
the Great Karoo Plain, a terrible dry stretch,
almost a desert: it took hours to pass through.
There were ostriches and butcher-birds and then
we were crawling round a narrow mountain ledge.
At last, after two days and nights on the train,
we arrived at Park Station, Johannesburg.

We were taken to Long's Hotel where we washed
and had a good breakfast; then Jack decided
to find some of his people. He didn't know
where anyone lived: they are all rolling stones.
But he knew that his niece, a girl of eighteen,
worked at a large draper's shop called Walter Wise,
so we went and found her. Her name was Edie.
She asked for the morning off, took us to meet
her mother, Jack's sister Ivy, then left to fetch
Jack's mother, who didn't seem pleased to see us;
next day, I also met Jack's sister Lily.
I summed them up as rather a funny crowd,

all living in furnished rooms: not one of them
had so much as a stick they could call their own.

I spent a couple of lonely days while Jack
went to one of the gold mines of the East Rand:
he was to start work the following Monday.
We set off for the nearest town, Benoni,
and found a place to live: an unfurnished room
with our own door and a piece of verandah.
Everything was so terribly expensive:
our furniture on the hire purchase system,
a Blue Flame Perfection stove to cook by,
a bicycle for Jack to ride to work on.
If it hadn't been for Jack's kind brother Frank,
who was on the railway in Natal and sent
£5 a month, we should never have pulled through:
from the start, I'd much to thank his brothers for.

One Sunday, after five months in Benoni,
we found that Jack's brother Bert was living there,
running a native eating house. We asked him
to supper: I made my table look lovely
for my first visitor. He was dark and tall,
quite different from Jack; he often popped in,
and persuaded us to take a house with him
in Bedford Street, with three rooms, kitchen, pantry,
bathroom, quite a nice back yard. Then Bert gave us
a present – half a dozen white Leghorn hens
and one rooster – so we'd plenty of fresh eggs.
For the first two months, we got on very well,
until Jack and Bert fell out: Bert decided
he was paying too much, which he was really –
we thought he was trying to help us along –
and so he packed his trunk and went, leaving us
in an awful stew. We had to find the rent,
light and water bills with no one to help out.
We put up a card: 'Unfurnished room to let'.

Within days a lady came and took the room:
a dressmaker, whose name was Mrs Vaughan.
She and her husband lost everything they had
in the diamond diggings. Just after that,
I was taken ill, my first baby was born,
but of course never lived. As Mrs Vaughan
had typhoid fever, Jack wired for his mother:
she came for a week and was quite kind to me.
Then Frank came to spend his three weeks' leave with us:
he took us to an auction mart, where we bought
sitting room chairs, sofa, and dining-table;
we went with him to cinemas and theatres
and, on the last Saturday, to the racecourse
at Germiston. I had never been before
and never since: it was all so exciting,
quite apart from the most delicious cold lunch
(I'm a pig, I always remember the food).

Frank went back, and soon after Jack's mother wrote:
her husband had left her and she was stranded,
so could she come and live with us? Jack and Bert
said they weren't going to have her in Benoni:
she'd disgrace them. So I asked them what they meant,
and they said: she gets drunk. She'd been kind to me,
so I persuaded them. Bert paid for her keep:
he'd now opened a fruit and grocery shop
with his profits from the Kaffir eating-house.
When the old lady had been with us a year,
she suddenly burst out with her drunkenness:
she'd got some money making milk-jug covers,
and one day two men brought her home in a cab.
She went back to Ivy in Johannesburg.
Bert sent her £1 a week: how she spent it,
on her living or on drink, I couldn't guess.

I'd now been in South Africa for two years,
and we were beginning to get on our feet.

We saved, I did lots of knitting and sewing,
until we had enough for a holiday:
we went to East London for Christmas, staying
with Jack's sister Millie. He had grown up there,
a lovely seaside place with a wonderful beach,
so he knew all about it. But, coming back,
there were lots of Cape policemen in the train:
it looked as though there'd be trouble on the Rand.
Benoni seemed the hottest spot. The miners
were out on strike, the surface men still working,
so Jack went back on Monday. Then they came out,
because the miners were threatening them. Of course,
a few turned up: the miners got hold of them
and thrashed them, while some men at Brakspan mines
were beaten and then thrown down a disused shaft.
Those miners were a proper unruly crowd,
mostly low Dutch, and not satisfied with that:
they broke into houses, tore down the curtains,
dragged out the furniture, set fire to the lot;
so many were left homeless in Benoni.

One morning, about the beginning of March,
we woke to bugles sounding the fall-in call:
it wasn't the Boy Scouts, it was the strikers
preparing for an imminent attack from
the Transvaal Scottish marching for Benoni.
A battle began, martial law was proclaimed,
nobody was allowed out after seven.
There were bullets whizzing up every street
and you daren't put your nose outside the door;
we had no food because the shops were all shut.
I was expecting Dulcie any minute.

Lily, better at recording death than birth,
has nothing to say about 23 March,
apart from a photo of a tree-lined street
and some low municipal buildings, captioned,
'Benoni, where Dulcie was born': my mother.

3

We had quite a houseful while we were shut up:
there were Mrs Vaughan, Bert, Mr Ashington –
they came for refuge while their shop was picketed –
as well as Jack and myself. But luckily
we had a sack of flour, so I could make bread:
no meat for days, just bread, tea and coffee.
We played cards and dominoes and tiddlywinks,
all the games we could think of. General Smuts
sent aeroplanes to drop bombs on us, and then
machine guns from aeroplanes, pop, pop, popping,
meaning to injure the miners but hurting
innocent people instead. Meanwhile, of course,
everyone was getting hungry: so, at night,
they looted the shops. Bert's was one of the first:
we could see men creeping along by the walls,
sacks full of stuff on their backs. And all the shops
in Market Avenue were treated the same,
boots, shoes and clothing as well as food taken,
and what they couldn't take broken or destroyed:
a town ruined, shops spoilt and houses riddled
with bullets, and ambulances tearing past.

It was a Monday morning when the strikers
were whacked: the place was filled with mounted police
and Transvaal Scottish when all of a sudden
a whole army of Free State Burghers appeared,
fierce funny-looking men, and they meant business.
They rounded up the men from every house:
they were driven in flocks like a lot of sheep
by these horrible old Dutchmen on horseback.
It was a boiling hot day, and some were sent
to the police station, while others were packed
into the athletic grounds in the hot sun,
a machine gun trained on them, nothing to eat
or drink. About 6.30 in the evening,
many were sent home, but the rest were detained.

The Beales were the happiest married couple:
they had a darling little boy named Jimmy,
their own house and car, everything they needed.
Mr Beale was detained for nothing at all:
his wife was ill, he was anxious to get back,
so at midnight he took off his boots, climbed out
the window, dodged the guards and was running home,
when he was challenged by some Transvaal Scottish.
He wouldn't stop, so they stabbed him through the heart
with a bayonet and, about the same time,
Mrs Beale had a baby daughter, Molly.
No one knew what had happened to Mr Beale
or where they buried him. When his wife told me,
I was in bed: Dulcie was then three days old,
a lovely fat baby with her dark blue eyes,
black hair, and a line right across her forehead,
just like May had when she cut her head open.

With the strike over, everyone was hard up.
Bert had lost everything and went to Jo'burg
to look for work. We moved to a smaller house,
four rooms and a scullery built in line,
with a wide mosquito-netted verandah,
a delightful place to sit and have our meals:
the floor was red stone with lots of plants in tubs,
a big table and two or three comfy chairs.
There was a gorgeous garden: along one side,
a run for our fowls and, along the other,
peach and plum trees, nectarines, quinces and vines;
in the middle, a lovely flower garden.
Dulcie slept in her pram beneath two peach trees:
she was six weeks when we moved from Bedford Street.
Our neighbours gave her a sweet little puppy,
a cross of Irish setter and Airedale named Pat:
he was a nuisance, but he loved the baby.

Things were still bad. Bert found no work in Jo'burg,
so came back to us: he did the gardening

and took baby out. Saturday afternoons,
we'd go to football: baby would be so good,
lying in the pram bought with my last £5.
And about this time Jack bought a motorbike,
a BSA, on the hire purchase system.
Finally, Bert got a job as manager
of a big store at Geduld Township in Springs,
so when he left us we had Millie and Frank
for their holiday, also Gladys and Gwen.
She is such a marm: she wanted waiting on –
of course, we couldn't afford a Kaffir boy –
and wouldn't lift a finger to do a thing.

A terrible storm began one afternoon,
starting at four o'clock and lasting six hours:
thunder, lightning, and hailstones big as golf balls.
It tore the leaves off the trees, killed the flowers,
and blocked up all the gutterings of the house.
Water streamed down the walls of every room,
wallpaper was torn off and furniture drenched;
I covered all the beds with mackintoshes
to keep them dry for the night. Well, that put an end
to our stay in the house: Jack was determined
we'd find a place that didn't let in water.
Bert persuaded us to move to Springs, near him,
where there were plenty of nice houses to let.

I decided before leaving Benoni
to give Pat back to his previous owners:
with a baby and a four-hour train journey,
I had quite enough to do. Gladys and Gwen
were coming with us too. We all got settled
on the train: it was just leaving the station,
when someone said, 'There's a dog under your seat.'
I looked; to my astonishment, there was Pat,
curled up. I hadn't got a ticket for him;
anyway, dogs had to travel in boxes;

but when the ticket collector came along,
Pat never budged an inch and so wasn't seen.
We had to change at Boksburg. Pat followed me
onto the train but wouldn't lie down again:
he paraded up and down the corridor.
I was told to put him off at the next stop,
but the ticket collector never returned,
and so poor old Pat got to Springs after all.

We were quite all right for a couple of months,
then Jack did a stupid thing. He'd served his time
as an apprentice, but his two years at war
meant he wasn't qualified to take a job
as a journeyman at six guineas a week;
they offered him an improver's job at five,
but he turned it down and said he'd look elsewhere.
That finished him: no mine would take him on now,
and that beastly motorbike from Benoni
wasn't paid for. All we'd saved was £15.
Gwen caught chickenpox and then Dulcie caught it:
she wasn't yet two and was very seedy.
To make matters worse, Gladys and Gwen moved out,
so we had to pay the rent of the whole house.

I was ill and we were down poverty street;
my third baby was born, and the poor mite lived
only eleven hours. We had no money
to pay for a doctor or the burial
of the little child: that bill is still owing
to this day. Jack had spent our last £15,
putting it down on a horse and cart: he said
he would sell vegetables for a living.
As time went on, he began to do quite well –
I really thought we would be able to pay
some of our debts – but in the middle of May
the mornings and evenings became very cold:
getting up early and going to market

didn't please the man. So all of a sudden,
he made up his mind to sell our little home
and make a trek to somewhere warmer: Durban.

Everything was sold at auction: those few pounds
we had to keep to feed us on the journey.
We couldn't pay any of our debts, so Jack
thought he might as well do somebody else down:
a few days before we set off, he ordered
a canopy for the cart, which made it look
like a covered wagon; he'd no intention
of paying for it. Bert threw up his good job
to join us. Otherwise, he said, we'd be killed:
one man couldn't manage a horse and wagon
on those treacherous hilly roads to Durban.
So we stole out like thieves early one morning,
without anyone knowing where we had gone.

4

A diary of our big trek, from Springs to Durban, a
distance of 483 miles, taking us exactly 30 days. By
one splendid horse named Polly and a covered trolley.
Started 5th June 1924
Finished 5th July 1924
Starting the journey: Bert, Jack, baby and myself, our
good old dog Pat and Miss Kitty.

Thursday 5th June: We leave Springs at 5.30,
and travel at a good trot, reaching Nigel
at 10.30: we outspan and make a fire
from dry cow dung, an excellent burning fuel,
and have a nice breakfast. We are ravenous,
eating two bacon rashers and two eggs each,
and almost a whole loaf of bread. Thus warmed up,
we all set to work: Bert feeds and grooms Polly,

while Jack and I wash up and put the cart straight.
We travel on to a place called Heidelberg,
arriving at 4.30, where we outspan
by the river. A kind man gives us some wood,
so we make a blazing fire and cook dinner
of grilled chops, wash the dishes and go to bed.
It's rather early and we find we can't sleep
for the strangeness and cold, though Dulcie sleeps well.

Friday 6th June: Bert is first up, makes a fire,
gets the kettle boiling by seven o'clock:
we have tea and toast, then make a good breakfast.
We walk through the town, a pretty little place,
a range of hills beyond and a white stone church,
a high bell tower and clock chiming the hour.
At eleven, we set off for Standerton:
a mile or two out, we strike a nasty hill
and we all have to help push with all our might.
After lunch, the road takes us through many farms
with big gates across the road. In the evening,
we find a lovely spot to camp for the night:
a stream for water, two hills to shelter us.

Saturday 7th June: Bert is up first again.
By about 9.30 we are on the road:
Jack and Bert try to get a few birds to eat,
while Dulcie and I go to sleep – surprising
how sleepy the jog of a cart makes one feel.
At midday, we rest and feed the good old horse,
then trot on, passing the village of Balfour,
and outspan for the night. Bert unpacks the cart,
Jack unharnesses Polly, gives her water,
while Dulcie and I look for some dry cow dung
to start a fire. Well, there isn't very much
just here. So we collect twigs, and then I think
of trying to get some coal from the railway.
As a train draws near, I hold up a small piece

I've found on the line: the driver and stoker
know just what I want and throw some large lumps out.
After a good meal, I put Dulcie to bed,
and then the three of us and our dog and cat
all sit round the lovely coal fire, and even
the good old horse comes trotting to take a look.

Sunday 8th June: We all wake up at sunrise
with the cooing of the doves. Jack is up first
and makes the fire, and we start off on our way
at half past nine. We cover a good distance,
as the road is flat passing through Greylingstad,
but there is no fresh water to be found here:
we have to use the emergency supply
which we always carry in a big stone jar.
When we reach a spring, we outspan for the night,
although it's still only early afternoon.
We have a good wash, and the men their first shave
since we left Springs: they need it very badly.
While we are eating our dinner this evening,
Polly strays and, after a lot of searching,
we find her trotting back the way we have come.

Monday 9th June: Glorious morning sunshine:
we travel hard until two o'clock. Water
is very scarce again, but at last we find
a beautiful river. We make up our minds
to go no further, for Polly needs a rest,
and I've got quite a lot of washing to do.

Tuesday 10th June: Horrors! Polly strays again.
Poor old horse, she may have been trotting all night.
After two hours' search, Bert finds her on a farm
three miles away. Half the morning being gone,
we decide to stop here until after lunch;
so I dry and air my washing on the grass,
mend a hole or two and sew some buttons on.

By dusk, we have reached the town of Standerton:
we find a delightful place to camp, sheltered
by tall blue gum trees, with the big River Vaal
running past us. Just as we're getting settled,
an elderly man and woman come rushing
across the field towards us: 'Get off our land!'
they both shout, but as soon as we speak they know
we aren't poor Dutch and they couldn't be more kind.
They ask us into their house and, when we leave,
give us new laid eggs and a huge jug of milk.

Wednesday 11th June: The old lady sends fresh milk
and hopes we've had a good night. After breakfast,
ready to leave, we find Miss Kitty has gone:
as a rule, she'd have been curled up on the cart
as soon as our blankets and cushions were on.
We had heard a tomcat strolling round the wood
in the night, so we go in there and call her:
Mr Tom comes running, but not Miss Kitty.
We decide to have a last look at the house,
and there she is, sitting on the verandah.
So we set off, passing many Kaffir kraals:
they are allowed to work on a farmer's land
for a quarter share of profits and they build
these pretty little round huts made of rushes,
with a hole for them to crawl through as a door,
like huge beehives. At last we reach Amersfoort,
where it's so bitterly cold and so windy
that baby and I have to stay in the wagon
while the men cook. We have a drop of brandy
to warm us up, but I swear that Jack and Bert
have more than that, for they're joking and laughing
all the time they cook. The dinner is A1.

Thursday 12th June: Kitty is missing again,
so we go on without her. I truly hope
she will find a nice home: she's such a sweet cat.

It is pretty here – there are lots of green trees,
plantations of blue gum trees border the road –
unlike most of the Transvaal, which is bare veldt.
Water is scarce: when we reach a little stream,
we outspan, as it's best to keep near water,
and then roast the wild doves that the men have shot.

Friday 13th June: Misty but not so cold.
An old Boer farmer comes up to chat with us:
we are firing at a target (my first shot
with a rifle, not bad for a beginner).
Then we are off: jogging along till midday,
a little rest, then on once more till sunset.
We outspan by a little stream near Volksrust,
but we don't manage a very good night's rest.
About one o'clock we look out: Polly has strayed.
Bert wakes up to find his mouth is frozen –
he's the coldest, sleeping under the wagon –
so Jack goes off to look for the horse. Meanwhile,
Bert lights our Primus stove and makes some cocoa
to warm us all up, for we're chilled to the bone.

Saturday 14th June: We are on the road
at quarter to ten, cars and traps passing us
on their way to morning market in Volksrust.
Jack takes the horse to be shod, we have our lunch,
then we start off once more: slow this afternoon,
as we have to climb steep hills. We see a train
on a narrow ledge cut into the hillside,
beneath the roadway. At last we travel down,
and camp in the valley where the three hills met,
beside a stream where ferns grow among the rocks.

Sunday 15th June: Fresh after a good night,
we are curious to learn what we shall find
on the other side of the enormous hill
which lies ahead of us. When we reach the top,
we pass through avenues of black wattle trees,

with lovely scent from mimosa-like flowers.
These pretty English-looking lanes take us past
Mujuba Hill, site of the famous battle
in the Boer War: up hill and down dale all day
through the most magnificent country I've seen,
until we reach a river sheltered by trees.

Monday 16th June: We decide to remain
in this ideal spot for the day. After breakfast,
Jack and Bert take the cartwheels off to soak them
in the river. Then we all have a good bathe
and wash our heads. Jack makes brake blocks for the cart,
for we'll soon be reaching some very steep hills,
while Bert, Dulcie and I wash our dirty clothes,
Kaffir-fashion, on the stones in the river.
We have a good dinner: we always eat well.

Tuesday 17th June: On the road once more,
lots of cars passing, fetching farmers to vote
in the nearest town, as it's election day.
Passing through mealie lands, we reach Newcastle
and find our river to outspan for the night.

Wednesday 18th June: Newcastle is busy
after the election as we walk through it.
When we return to the wagon, Pat has gone:
we at last find him wandering round the town
and so start again on our way until dusk.

Thursday 19th June: A bitterly cold night
and an uneventful day. At Danhauser,
where we outspan, there is no grass for Polly:
a poor dry place, but we make the best of it.
Before we go to bed, a boy comes along
and offers to have the horse in his paddock.

Friday 20th June: Up early this morning,
buying food in the village: the cheapest place

we have struck, and everyone seems so friendly.
Through the morning, we travel on even ground –
so even that I take the reins for a time –
before we hit some terrible rocky roads.
In fact, they aren't roads at all, just baboon paths,
a mass of rocks and stones winding round the hills.

Saturday 21st June: Once we are off,
we have more terrible monkey paths to climb.
We outspan for the night inside some farm gates:
it's so warm this evening that I can sit out
beside the camp fire and write two letters home.

Sunday 22nd June: A dusty road
this morning: we pass a coal mine, Kaffir kraals,
then a lot of Boer War graves near Ladysmith.
The town itself we find is rather pretty,
road and railway in the valley, and houses
all built on the hillsides. We stay for the night
on a common full of mimosa bushes.

Monday 23rd June: Polly must be shod,
so Jack takes her into town. We start trekking
again after lunch, but all of a sudden
a terrific wind gets up: we have to stop
and camp there in some very sandy quarters.

Tuesday 24th June: A terrible night,
the wagon almost blown over in the wind
and sand flying about in all directions:
at daybreak, we get away from that desert
but not out of that wind. We reach Colenso.

Wednesday 25th June: Our luck is out:
an awful night with a wicked thunderstorm
and only a few spots of rain. However,
about seven in the morning it rains hard:
we stay put until it clears at eleven.

The dear old sun shines again. After shopping,
we go off the main road to take a short cut,
very close to the border of Zululand.
We pass a tribe of men going to battle,
youngest to oldest, all armed, with their war paint,
assegais and shields: I suppose they've quarrelled
and are going to fight it out. From our camp,
we hear in the distance a native wedding:
they sing all the time for three days and three nights.
It is such a ghastly noise: their throats must ache.

Thursday 26th June: A lovely morning:
the wind drops, the sun is beautifully warm.
And birds: canaries galore! Well, off we go,
through pretty country, but such a rocky road,
and all uphill. Target practice after lunch:
I beat both the men. We wonder when we'll strike
the main road, and we tell ourselves we'll never
take short cuts again, for they take twice as long.
At sunset, we meet the road: after a mile,
we find a good spot to outspan for the night.
Everyone we speak to, even Kaffir boys,
marvels at our willing and wonderful horse,
who's pulled us and our load all the way from Springs.

Friday 27th June: The road is nice and smooth,
so Polly starts at a good pace. We soon reach
Estcourt, where our best bacon and sausages
come from, a lovely little place with clean streets.
Jack goes to the shop to buy mealies and bran
for Polly's feed. We have a terrible hill
to climb from this town: it seems never-ending.
We find some water, stop a couple of hours,
then up more hills on a pass cut round the side.
The sun shines down on gorgeous flowers and ferns,
hillsides above us, water rushing below.
We outspan by a blue gum tree plantation.

Saturday 28th June: At every bend,
we find we have to climb higher still, until
at last we reach the top and a steep road down.
We're quite near the end of this when Polly trips
and begins to limp. We stop and bathe the knee,
before moving on to find a resting-place:
this is Mooi River, and the little town
named after it is noted for its butter.

Sunday 29th June: We have our breakfast,
without hurrying, so that Polly can rest.
While we are sitting there, a chicken turns up:
it's the only one about and it's so tame
that Jack decides we'll have to take it with us.
We haven't anything to eat for dinner,
and as it's a Sunday the shops will be shut.
What a wicked thing to do! Yet on the road,
it seems as though it were a gift from the gods,
knowing that we should go hungry otherwise.
So we set off again with more hills to climb:
cows and sheep grazing on their sides, and below,
a stream between plantations of black wattle.
We outspan for the night in a sheltered spot,
then make a fire and roast the little chicken
in our good three-legged Kaffir cooking-pot:
a delicious meal, though stolen property.

Monday 30th June: It seems so funny:
although the drop is almost 6,000 feet
from Johannesburg to the sea at Durban,
we are always going uphill. However,
at last the road is getting fairly level
as we pass through very English-looking lanes
to reach the pretty health resort of Howick,
which is famous for its lovely waterfalls.
Here I see oranges, lemons and nartjies
(tangerines at home) growing for the first time.

We find a nice place to camp by the river,
but the grass is rather long and I'm afraid
of meeting a snake, even though the men say
they will never show themselves in the winter.

Tuesday 1st July: There are many more trees
growing in Natal: everything is so green.
Hydrangeas are growing wild on the hillsides,
and aloes with fibrous trunks, watery leaves,
red flowers at the top. We have to go down
a tremendous hill to Pietermaritzburg:
we are coming level with the railway line,
a train with three engines steaming towards us.
There are big houses in beautiful gardens,
looking tropical, with bamboos and huge palms,
and plenty of well-dressed people. What a state
of excitement Dulcie is in: such a change
from the veldt and hills! She's never seen a tram
until now. On the other side of the town,
we find a good place to outspan for the night.

Wednesday 2nd July: Lovely and fresh,
with another hill to climb: flat road after that.
It's so hot, we have to rest by a river
for two or three hours before carrying on
to flatter land with fields and fields of mealies,
and a few of barley or wheat, nice and green
between the yellow mealies. We are quite late
on the road, as we haven't found water:
we trot on, through clouds of warm and then cold air,
but still no water. Entering Camperdown,
Bert asks a Zulu boy to fetch us water:
he brings us two bucketsful, and new laid eggs
at a shilling a dozen. After dinner,
it's warm enough for us to sit without coats
for the first time since we began our journey.

Thursday 3rd July: One more tremendous hill;
on the other side, blue gum tree plantations
being hewn down, as far as the eye can see.
We come to 'The Valley of a Thousand Hills',
and then another climb: this road is a ledge
turning round and round the hill, with no water.
At dusk, we come across some road repairmen,
four whites, several natives: the whites are drunk.
They won't give us water, but they offer drink
to Bert and Jack, who refuse: they are horrid,
and I'm really quite scared. So we carry on,
reaching a place called Hillcrest: there is water
from the power station and we have our meal,
then after a long day settle for the night.

Friday 4th July: We find a lovely spot,
a precious stream and wonderful shady trees,
where we have a bathe and do all the washing;
for we're nearing Durban, the end of our trek.
We remain here until about four o'clock,
then travel on: there are bananas,
pineapples and paw paw; fields of sugar cane
stretching for miles. Close to an Indian school,
we stop for the night, with the lights of Durban
and the lighthouse flickering in the distance.

Saturday 5th July: Just before we leave,
the Indian schoolmaster brings us a bowl
of freshly picked oranges. Hundreds of cars
are passing us on their way to Durban races
for the July Handicap, so on we trot,
all the way to the racecourse and outspan there,
like gypsies at the Derby, and watch the race.
In the evening, Bert takes me to see Durban,
while Jack looks after Dulcie, who is asleep.
We take a tram to the beach – it is high tide,
huge breakers coming over the esplanade –

then back in a rickshaw, a rubber-tyred cart
with a barefooted Kaffir boy pulling us.
He is dressed to kill: a pair of bullock's horns
stuck on his head, decorated with feathers
and flowers, and a goatskin round his shoulders.
Eventually we arrive back at our home,
the wagon, and have our usual good night's sleep.

5

Next day, we travelled up the coast of Natal,
close to the mouth of the Umgeni River,
where we found a place to camp on a sand-dune,
bushy trees forming a half-circle round us,
a salt water pool – the Blue Lagoon – in front,
and the great Indian Ocean beyond it.
We spent all July out in the open there,
leading a healthy bushman's life, with free rent,
free wood, free water, catching fish, shooting birds:
it really is the way we were meant to live.
But we knew that soon we'd have to find a home.

Eventually, we found two unfurnished rooms
in a house shared with some Malayan people.
The floors were stone, and we had no furniture:
we had to put the mattresses on the floor,
and make the best of it. We tethered Polly
on a piece of nearby ground; within a week,
she got free and broke her leg. We had her shot.
I felt dreadful: she had been a faithful friend
and worked hard. Bert went back to Johannesburg
to find a job: he had been a good friend too.
Jack sold the wagon for only a few pounds
to help us along until he could find work.
Dulcie became ill with a high temperature.
I got rheumatism in my feet and legs –

it was sleeping on the stone floor, I suppose –
and couldn't put on my shoes. We all had colds.
Dulcie recovered, though she did look seedy,
but I couldn't walk and Jack didn't bother:
he made no effort at all to find a job.

I'd struggle to the verandah for fresh air
and watch people waiting for trams to Durban.
One morning a man called down to me and said:
'I've seen you there for weeks and can't understand
why you're living in a coloured person's house.
It isn't done here. Are you in need of help?'
I said I'd give anything to get away,
but we had nothing. He promised to call in:
he worked for the Governor General Fund.

When I told Jack what I'd done, he wasn't pleased.
But I said we couldn't go on living there,
in that damp place, without a bed to lie on,
nor a table or chair, while he did nothing
to get us out of the mess. When the man came,
he was horrified. He told Jack he'd help us
get back to Johannesburg and, next morning,
he'd take Dulcie and me to the Fund's office.
So Jack wrote then and there to Bert, asking him
to find us a room, and the following morning
the man hired a rickshaw for Dulcie and me
(in Jack's bedroom slippers) to go to the Fund.
There they said that they would send for us again
as soon as we heard Bert had found us a room.
A week later, he wrote to say he had done so:
in a suburb of Jo'burg called Wolhuter,
with a German woman, Mrs Robertson.
He'd also bought us beds, as he couldn't bear
the thought of us sleeping on the floor again.
I went to the Governor General Fund
and told them: they had railway and food tickets

for Jack and me, but there weren't baby tickets,
so the man gave me £1 from his pocket
to buy her food. What kindness from a stranger!

Our new room was spotlessly clean, with bare boards,
two iron beds and curtains at the window.
Mrs Robertson lent us table and chairs
until we could buy our own. Such poverty!
We had only a couple of pounds for food;
Bert had paid our first month's rent. Every midday,
this sweet German woman brought Dulcie a meal.
She had two little boys: when they had their lunch,
Dulcie had hers too. Jack's only comment was:
'Anyone would think I can't afford her food.'
I replied: 'You can't, and she can't take pot luck
like us.' At last my feet were getting better:
I could put my own shoes on again. But Jack
still hadn't found work, although he was looking.
By now, even my wedding ring had been pawned:
I used to sit and think how silly I'd been
to leave England for this place, and then I'd think
I couldn't have been so terribly wicked
that God would want me and my baby to starve.
We had been there a month and the rent was due.
A few days later, a letter came from home:
Dad, sensing all wasn't well, enclosed five pounds,
a tidy sum for him, a godsend for us.

Then Jack got a job with the Parks Department:
not what he wanted, though better than nothing.
It was good to get back to normal living,
a weekly wage coming in, and every week
we managed to buy some piece of furniture:
we started going to auction rooms again.
Jack met a few friends while we were living there:
a blacksmith, Fred Holton, and Eileen Goldsmith,
an old girlfriend of his. But after six months,

he decided we should move into Jo'burg,
nearer his work. He found an unfurnished room
in Bree Street, at the bottom of the garden
of a big house: he preferred his own front door.
He soon got fed up with gardening and said
he was sure that he could make a tea-room pay:
so he borrowed the money from Fred Holton
to rent a shop at the top end of Bree Street.
He fixed it up with a few tables and chairs,
a counter for fruit and sweets and cigarettes,
and then we duly opened. I worked and worked
to keep the place clean, even cleaning windows,
which was something a white woman never did.
There weren't many customers. I did breakfasts
for the rooms over the shop, just tea and toast,
and each morning I used to take the trays up;
we sold quite a lot of sweets and cigarettes,
but no teas or coffees, where the money was.

After four months, we couldn't pay the warehouse:
in desperation, I wrote to Bert for help.
He came on the night train to Johannesburg,
took one look at the books and said: 'You must go:
just pack a few things and do a moonlight flit.'
He went for Jack for being such a wastrel:
why couldn't he work and keep his wife and child
in a proper manner? He told us to leave
Saturday night by the Pretoria train,
change for Naboomspruit, wait till Monday,
then take the train to where he worked at Crecy:
it was just a little halt among large farms,
on the border of Southern Rhodesia.
Bert ran the huge corrugated iron store,
with everything from a needle to a plough,
also post office and telephone exchange:
alongside, there was a bedroom, living-room,
and improvised kitchen; no water or light.

There were oil lamps; water was fetched from a well
two hundred yards away, in paraffin tins,
by Martin the native boy, on a barrow.
So this was the place that we were going to.

6

At last we were aboard the train to Crecy,
a little Puffing Billy kind of engine
and three trucks – one for whites and two for coloureds –
with forms on either side and canvas flapping:
it ran twice a week, the days for meat and mail.
So we jolted along through miles of rough veldt,
all very dry and dusty, until we reached
the Crecy siding. A hundred yards away
stood the huge iron store. We got settled in.
Bert told Jack what to do: he would get £5
a month, which wasn't much but was his to save,
because our food and clothing would come from stock
and Bert would pay from his share of the profits.
I learnt to run the post office for train days:
it seemed as though the world and his wife arrived
from all the farms round about, in mule carts, cars,
or with ox wagons. We had to shut the shop
while we sorted the mail; then they'd all swarm in
to get their letters, stamps and postal orders.

The rest of the week we only had a few
straggling natives: they'd walk miles from their kraals,
buy a pair of boots, then walk a little way
and take them off again, tie them together,
sling them over their shoulders and go barefoot.
One day a boy came in to buy a blanket:
Bert spent three hours getting every blanket
off the shelves, then he said he didn't want one.
Bert went for him in his Basuto language,

clicking his tongue, until one of his false teeth
flew out of his mouth and over the counter.
The boy was terrified: he ran from the shop,
screaming and yelling and expecting the tooth
to pursue him. That settled the argument.
We had a good laugh, folding up the blankets.

Some of the people who came in on mail days
used to invite Dulcie and me to their farms.
I also became quite friendly with the girl
on the Naboomspruit telephone exchange,
although I'd never seen her; we would discuss
gramophone records. She'd put on the latest,
and play it through the telephone: 'Tea for Two',
'Valencia', 'I'll Be Loving You Always'.

At the tennis court near the railway siding,
farmers would come and play: we made a foursome
with our nearest neighbour, Captain Sanderson.
He lived alone in a farmhouse with his boy,
Franz, to do for him: it was a pretty place,
made from two rondavels for the two main rooms.
I also kept chickens for an interest,
starting with a dozen hens and a rooster.
I never cooped them up: they wandered the veldt,
eating grubs and insects, but came home to roost
at night, when I gave them a good feed of corn.
There was one white hen the men had named Lily:
they said she took after me, spruce and fussy;
if she could get into my bedroom, she would,
and then lay her egg on my bed. However,
after a time I shut the door and window:
then she laid her eggs under a mimosa,
where we couldn't reach and, having laid thirteen,
sat on them and brought out thirteen lovely chicks.
There was one little chick that would lag behind,
so poor old Pat (we still had him) used to go
and help it with a gentle push from his paw.

One day, a hawk swooped and caught this little one,
but Lily flew up and fought till he dropped it:
I put Vaseline on it and cared for it,
and it was fit again in a day or two.
One by one my hens were all going broody:
I called one, a busybody, Mrs Dixon,
while Milly was easy and comfortable,
and in the end I had hundreds of chickens.

We had a plague of locusts like a black cloud:
they settled on Captain Sanderson's mealie,
just coming up, and ate all the young green shoots.
They were horrible-looking things, and their wings
made an unbelievable noise when they flew.
Then there were ants. White ones would eat through a sack
in a night and right through our carpet as well;
black ones, bigger than in England, really bite
if they get on you, and there's a big red ant.
After it had rained, they all grew wings and flew
until their wings dropped off, and then you'd find them
crawling around. And such huge spiders that sting!
I met some very strange insects at Crecy.

The siding further up from us was Truro:
Harry and Lily Lawe managed a farm there.
He was something to do with the Scout movement,
and one weekend he went to Johannesburg
for a dinner honouring Baden Powell,
who was visiting South Africa just then.
He didn't like to leave his wife in the farmhouse,
surrounded by native kraals, so he asked me
to spend the weekend with her. Dulcie and I
caught the little train to Truro one Friday:
it was quite a treat to live in a real house,
well furnished with lovely kitchen and bathroom.
They had five Alsatians, Molly and Roland,
and three puppies: Dulcie loved them and they her.
We slept with revolvers under our pillows,

and were very glad we had them and the dogs,
for we were the only white people for miles.
Friday was quiet; Saturday and Sunday,
the natives got drunk on beer – the noise they made
was quite eerie at times, and we were both pleased
to see Harry step off the train on Monday.
We caught its return journey, back to Crecy.

There was a whirlwind: we could see it coming
miles away, picking up the dry sandy earth.
We went into the shop and shut all the doors,
but the wind took my improvised kitchen –
pots, pans, kettles, basins, teacloths, everything –
and blew it over the veldt. When it died down,
we had to go searching for our belongings;
the air was stifling, with a smell of red sand
for days, until eventually the rains came.

Martin brought a baby jackal for Dulcie:
he was such a nice boy and so fond of her,
and he thought that she would like him as a pet.
He was a little grey fluffy animal,
with a pointed nose, and he loved being nursed,
but as he grew older he became spiteful;
we couldn't put up with bites from his sharp teeth,
so we took him for a walk to Twee Kopjes,
where there were jackals (we could hear them at night),
and let him go back to his natural friends.

1926. And there the journal ends:
blank white pages in a black-covered notebook
conceal Jack's rages and Lily's departure;
her funding a passage home (Bert helped, of course)
by working at the Singer sewing machine
in the attic above me now; her return
to London and her going into service
at Overstrand Mansions – a single mother,
with a four-year-old daughter – in Battersea.

Parkland

As far as the eye can see:
stately white-painted railings;
cropped grass darkened here and there
by tactful underground streams;
chestnuts, birches, oaks fenced off
or, nearer home, encircled
by slatted wooden benches;
and, in the shadowed distance,
conversational horses.

It stretches back to childhood,
a scattered Surrey village:
cattle-grids and gravelled tracks
made the contours of my map;
a wilderness half-contained,
organic and orderly,
trying out its boundaries,
asserting its clarity.
I have always loved parkland.

The Break

Woodsmoke and dusk can always bring it on,
That September evening fifty years ago:
Absurd in my crisp new suit from Horncastle's,
A starched white collar and a silly striped tie,
Pretending I was something I wasn't quite yet.

The road through Godstone, Oxted, Westerham;
At Riverhead, the church perched on its hill;
A long town, yew trees and a gravelled drive;
Unloading cars and big uncurtained windows;
Inside, a crush of notice-boards and scurrying.

Then, snatched goodbyes in the hessian-covered hall.
I should have said: 'I'm not staying here.
These people are mad. We're going home.'
My mother would have said: 'You know he's right.'
And my father: 'If you're sure that's what you want …'

The grey Wolseley would have swept over the gravel,
Through the gates, down Tubs Hill, into open country;
Lit villages would have glowed with benediction,
And soon we'd have been home, laughing and weeping
Over a scratch supper of bacon and eggs.

Instead, towards the middle of second prep
Each evening, I'd imagine them sitting down
To dinner, and my empty place at the table,
With a vase, perhaps, or a wine bottle or the cruet
To fill the space where my own plate should have been.

One wrong turning can mess up all your life.
It's taken fifty years to see that this was it,
The break that left me forever disconnected.
I hoped that it would all come right at Christmas,
With presents or prayer, but of course it never did.

The Lindshammar Pig

This glassblower's cheeks are bulbous as Dizzy Gillespie's
As he forms what must surely be a blue glass flask.
He'll add four feet, two ears, blob eyes, a curly tail,
And seal the aperture to create a stumpy snout.

But in truth he's ruined it: that slit along the back
Turns it into a piggy-bank, a glowing deep-blue toy.
'It would be great as a pig, without the slit,' says the boy.
'Okay' – and the glassblower smiles – 'for you I make one.'

We have come to Vetlanda, in the east of Sweden,
By slow train from cabbage-coloured Gothenburg,
Steaming in a warm wet summer. Some long hours later,
The pig is boxed and cotton-woolled, safe for its journey.

Caught in a North Sea storm, the ferry runs six hours late;
His mother brings the seasick boy a peach, then eats it.
Asked at Tilbury Customs, 'Anything to declare?'
The boy replies winningly: 'Yes, I have a blue pig.'

Now the Lindshammar pig surveys a Suffolk snowfield
And everybody from that day in Vetlanda is dead,
Except for the boy and, in a manner of speaking, the pig.
If there's an afterlife, the glassblower will be smiling.

A Huntingdonshire Elegy

in memory of Rod Shand

How typical of you to disappear like that:
Nothing packed, wallet and house-keys left,
Just going for a stroll. So here's a caveat:

A double existence out of Greene or le Carré
Is something you might plausibly possess.
Your life's disguises seem to twinkle: 'Solve me!'

You were a riddle from the day I heard of you,
Bored, out of my depth, at my first staff meeting,
Where dull men grumbled on about no one I knew.

'What does one say to a boy who spends his summer
Touring the brothels of Latin America?'
Silence, then: 'Ask for the addresses, Headmaster.'

This I must meet, I thought. And luck had me teaching
'General English' to the upper science sixth,
As if someone supposed they needed civilising.

Some did; but you, the biologist from Bogotá,
Introduced me to your Spanish talisman,
The 'Pequeño Poema Infinito' of Lorca.

At Christmas and Easter, though it seemed illegal,
You didn't go home but took a flat in Cambridge.
We roamed the colleges, drank in the Eagle,

And talked and talked of books. One afternoon you
Inscribed to me your first edition Márquez:
'Winner of the Shand Peace Prize, 1972.

'Love, Roddy.' Now I picture you in Staughton,
Purple tee-shirted, sprawled in my Lurashell chair,
Urgently telling me what next to fix my mind on,

Or in Colombian poncho at the thatched Crown
('Good evening, duckie,' grinned a friendly old local);
A few days afterwards, the little pub burnt down.

In your interview to read Marine Biology
At Queens', you said you'd sooner go to Bangor.
'Why?' they asked, aghast. 'Because it's got some sea.'

Land of my fathers! I thought of you at the edge
Of your academic ocean, nursing draught Guinness
When you rang from a pub across the Menai Bridge,

Or writing long letters from Neuadd Emrys Evans –
I treasured that name's triple-decker Welshness –
On marine secrets: tomato pips and waste remains.

Next you were off to the Susversity of Unisex
To work on your doctorate: when we met in Lewes
I sensed – was it boredom or something more complex?

Hard to tell, but the thesis remained unfinished.
One chilly Easter week, we went to Aldeburgh,
My own adopted coast. And then you vanished.

It was years before I heard from you again,
Until, on a May evening, there you were in Derby,
Once more feeding coins into a greedy pub phone:

Married, working for British Rail, and worrying
(You said) about your Guinness getting cold.
This seemed both unexpected and unsurprising,

True to a form I was beginning to understand:
So when you and Judy moved to Silicon Valley,
A plush village address in Berkshire commuter-land,

No doubt I should have guessed that it wouldn't last.
An unexplained resurfacing at St Andrews, Malta,
Seemed altogether more your style. Years passed.

Then you were running a restaurant in Vancouver
And doing some part-time teaching at the aquarium.
But was this a reinvention or a cover?

It's early summer: perhaps in that other life you're
Sipping a cocktail now in Montreal or Moscow,
As the scent of beanfields wafts over Staughton Moor.

Kenpas Highway, 1966

Steady rain, and the wipers' shuffling beat
Smudges streetlamps and the passing cars
Into a slurry of extruded light.
The city centre with its crowds and bars –
Down to the next junction, then turn right –
Seems as remote and washed-out as the stars.

And so at Kenilworth Road, the signals red,
I hug the nearside lane, the way I'll go
Back to my silent digs and narrow bed;
While Jimmy Ruffin on the radio
Wonders what becomes of the broken-hearted.
I think I could tell him that. I think I know.

For first love never disappears: it sets,
A pearl one neither loses nor forgets.

Blackborough Park

1

At the bus stop by the iron gates, a man steps off
The green double-decker, which trundles away.
He turns towards the park. Ahead, low in the sky,
A sun red as a chilblain glares down on him
And the grubby gravel path bisecting the grass
With its molehills, wormcasts and black muddy edge.

He's a man you've seen before: the kind of man
Who steps off double-deckers, whether green or not,
Wearing a fawn-coloured mac or a dark overcoat,
Balding on top though needing a haircut next week
To sort out that whiskery stuff round his neck and ears,
With scuffed shoes, a scruffy look, up to no good.

Soon the path branches, as he remembers it should.
The right-hand fork climbs towards formal gardens,
South-facing against the north wall and, further along,
Some overgrown allotments. Now he remembers
Brash massed dahlias, yearning michaelmas daisies.
His father brought him here on Saturday mornings.

The left fork dips down into a long shaded avenue:
Wellingtonias or (he searches for the proper word) sequoias,
Century-old striplings, yet already rubbing shoulders.
He chooses this path, despite the autumnal chill;
He likes the way in which sunlight turns to starlight,
Glinting through the leaves and dancing on the ground.

Down there, he thinks, where the avenue ends there's a lake:
He'd feed the ducks, and one summer a pair of swans
Appeared, paraded round, and were never seen again.
But it was late September when, walking home from school,
They dared Richard Bell to swim across and he drowned.
And from that day on the park was out of bounds.

2

At the opposite gate, almost half a mile away,
There's a girl in a striped woolly scarf, pushing a pram:
A proper old-fashioned pram, with a recurrent squeak
From its nearside rear wheel like a plaintive cat,
And within it a baby in an Edwardian bonnet,
Dozing with an air of perplexed tranquillity.

This is strange and not strange: it matches the park,
Which itself seems forged from the indeterminate past.
And the girl herself, despite those horizontal stripes
On the scarf wrapped round and round her long dark hair,
Is a patchwork sort of person; fragments of pattern,
Paisley or Morris, peep from beneath her coat.

If you imagine her house, it has multicoloured rugs,
Hand-embroidered cushions, home-made curtains;
She reads with unfashionable taste – Elizabeth Bowen,
Ivy Compton-Burnett – and cooks well with organics,
Wholefoods; she's a cheerfully lapsing vegetarian.
It is less easy to imagine her husband or partner.

She walks to where paths meet at a tall thin lamppost.
'Pole,' says the child, suddenly waking and staring:
A random first word, perhaps, or an accurate observation.
'Pole,' she repeats dreamily, mostly to herself. 'That's right.'
They are going downhill now, away from the gazebo,
Towards the circle with an obelisk, close to the lake.

She pauses to absorb the sunlit scene around her,
Pointing things out to the child, who nevertheless
Remains obstinately entranced by the gesturing finger.
One day she'll explain how the words round the obelisk
Record the gift of Sir Alfred Blackborough, this park,
In memory of his only son, killed at Mafeking.

3

On the park's north boundary there's an undulating wall,
A crinkle-crankle wall they'd call it in East Anglia,
And, midway along, a narrow latched wooden door,
Through which Alice might enter her garden of talking flowers;
Although, on the other side, there's an urban back lane,
Rusty bikes and wheelie bins, washing-lines in yards.

The boy in the leather jacket sneaks in with the air
Of someone seeking a quiet windless spot for a fag,
Away from his nagging parents and scrounging sister.
The jacket is ripped – tufts of red lining show through –
And his jeans are stained with blotches of motor oil,
Which is curious for someone who can't afford a car.

He sets off along the little path where in spring
There's an alpine garden and a shady drift of bluebells;
Now there are remnants of colchicum, autumn crocus,
But he doesn't notice them. This segment of the park
Has relics of allotments: a clump of artichokes,
A gnarled tree stooping with its load of small apples.

He doesn't notice because noticing is not what he does:
Clear and purposeful, he would, if he thought about it,
Regard looking and imagining as beside the point.
He's just split with his girlfriend, who's still only fifteen,
And therefore illegal, so it's probably just as well.
He cuts across the cropped grass towards the gazebo.

The gazebo is closed and boarded-up for the winter:
There are torn posts advertising discos, gigs, a circus;
Some bloke from the BNP has put one there as well.
The boy in the leather jacket doesn't stop to read them:
Without so much as a glance, he nips round the back
And in the urine-scented shade he lights his cigarette.

4

An old lady sits on the knobbly, uncomfortable bench
By the lakeside. The sun, livid and low to her right,
Casts long spiky shadows from nearby leafless trees.
Wrapped up against the cold in a cream woollen coat
And on her head a two-storey cake-shaped hat,
She looks like a chess-piece, the White Queen perhaps.

A quartet of mallards sidles up, with expectant quacks.
She smiles at them helplessly. 'I've nothing for you,'
She tells them, making a forlorn empty-hands gesture.
The ducks paddle off, quite seeming to understand,
Only to dither, circle and return: short-term memory
Possibly not their strong point nor, she concedes, hers.

Indignant at this, she shouts at them fiercely: 'Shoo!'
And they indeed sort of disperse, as she turns
Away from the lake, to glance back along the path
Where a girl pushes a pram as, many years ago,
She did, when the park was young. She smiles once more
At the overlapping image, this strange turning of time.

She thinks: it's an old-fashioned pram, a proper pram,
And it wants a drop of oil. A boy in a leather jacket
Grinds a cigarette butt into the path near the gazebo,
While a man in mac or overcoat suddenly emerges
Into sunlight from the shadowed avenue. She thinks:
They'll all meet at the obelisk. I wonder what will happen.

What happened? Well, of course, I wasn't there,
And can't be expected to know. This is infuriating
But, unlike most things in this story, true. As for the man
From the double-decker bus, the girl with the pram,
The boy in the leather jacket, the old lady on the bench,
The ducks she didn't feed. They were there. They were.

Strand, 1923

No shadows here: the distance recedes in mist;
A London Particular's inching up the river.
Crowds fill the pavement and the open-topped buses.
One or two of them have read *The Waste Land*.

A poster: 'Break any engagement to see *Ambush*.'
Another suggests a trip to *Little Old New York*.
Handbag beneath her arm, clothes unshowy but good,
Mrs Dalloway passes the Strand Palace Hotel.

And no one has noticed the photographer –
Except from the back of a horse-drawn covered wagon,
Propped among sacks and packages, the grocer's boy
Smiles shyly at the camera and the future.

Louis Takes a Break

Meanwhile, elsewhere: in Richmond, Indiana,
Seven musicians huddle round a horn
Which, like the Strand's unnoticed camera,
Records the moment. Yes, a star is born.

Because the second cornet's so majestic,
They've put him at the back where he won't drown
Honoré's trombone or Johnny's blackstick;
A wise move, that, until those chimes ring down.

Then something happens: Louis takes a break.
The hot news from America fills our ears:
A sound too proud and noble to mistake,
Through all the wow and flutter of the years.

At the Piano

June 1/64. To S/H Grand Piano in Rosewood Case by Cramer. £140–0–0

1

Facing familiar letters, inlaid, uppercase –
CRAMER LONDON – I glimpse their burnished gold
Gleaming in a showroom. The year is 1912.

Grand double doors admit potential buyers.
Will they affront the air with dissonance from Vienna?
Or risk some ragtime? No, tryers-out play safe,

Meandering through a simple drawing-room ballad,
Wrestling with Chopin, ending with Chopsticks.
A show-off might tinker with Rachmaninov.

The men carry hats, the ladies parasols. Outside,
New Bond Street is sunlit, great wars unimagined.
And the piano, unflappable as a salesman, sings.

2

A period of use, long years of beauty sleep,
Then restoration in a Kentish village.
It's the last straw for the piano-tuner's wife:
'George, if you don't get rid of it, I'm leaving.'

Their little house is rattling with pianos –
This one, his favourite, clogging up the garage.
Almost in tears, he sells it to my father,
Who says it will be used (his son is learning).

3

It's taken half a lifetime and a death
To reunite us both: my piano and I.

And the music: *Master Series for the Young,*
The Eclipse Series of Artistic Albums …

My piano-teacher's tactful fingerings
No longer fit these same but different hands.

His pencilled dates assert my competence
At this baffling Beethoven in 1963.

Well, I must practise, try at last to grasp
What once I understood imperfectly.

4

One friend disputes the sovereignty of keys.
I counter with the obvious example:
A sonata's plangent song of C sharp minor
Transposed a semitone down to C just dies.

But what about the moonlight rivalry,
Debussy's all flats and Beethoven's all sharps,
Same notes to play yet given different names
And therefore sounding different: how can that be?

No less incongruous, the shock of sameness:
That dour A flat supporting middle C
Which starts the *Pathétique's* adagio
Is the first chord of Ellington's 'Mood Indigo'.

5

Sometimes at night I hear a ghost-piano
Played by Winifred Atwell or Russ Conway,
Its out-of-tuneness a reproachful echo;

Or else recall my teacher's old black Bechstein,
The ivories scabbed and ridged like fingernails,
The treble sweet as Rubinstein's or Curzon's.

At other times, the dream-perspective alters
And views the instrument on a different scale:
Beneath the lid, a gym for tiny creatures

Who vault over the dampers, safely landing
On soft blue felt before they scale the pegs.
How did anyone imagine such a thing?

6

Piano Malcolm frowns: ill-tempered clavier.
Its sins no worse than age and wilfulness,
It hates the central heating and the weather.

Now Malcolm tells me that my piano's thirsty:
He prescribes a bowl of water underneath.
The cat looks puzzled, then laps gratefully.

Proof of Identity

What he kept showed what he was: passports,
Wartime identity card, rare photographs
Snapped on his business travels or, much later on,
As a tired and portly district councillor.

He'd be leaving for home: polishing his shoes,
Checking his silk tie, kissing his wife goodbye;
A dewy garden carnation in his buttonhole,
His handkerchief folded to its alpine peak.

Or returning: *News* and *Standard* flung aside,
Reaching for the decanter, the evening's first sherry,
Smelling of the world and his smoky journey home –
The last steam train from London Bridge to Reigate.

Then he'd be away for days or weeks at a time,
Piecing together Europe's shattered glassware,
His passports crammed with kaleidoscopic visas;
The People's Republic of Yugoslavia takes a page.

It's Belgium and Holland mostly: his closest friends
The Wautys and the Dehandschutters of Manage,
And always, in Maastricht, the Mager Brothers
Who sounded, I thought, like something out of films.

And surely Willy Mager took these photographs,
In their continental treacle-tinted colour:
My father relaxed, ironic, in command,
Looking for once the statesman he should have been.

My mother's with him (I'm packed off at school),
More beautiful and happier than I remember her
On the emotional see-saw of our life at home.
It strikes me now that she's in love: with whom?

Unanswerable still. She stayed loyal to her man,
The father I've come too late to understand,
As I rummage through these remnants of identity:
His passports, a few photographs, and me.

Hotel Codan

With its perkily assertive fifties lowercase 'd',
The hotel's sign has just gone out of date.
Otherwise, it's as the man from Tuborg said:
All glassy restraint, and the best view in town.

I must earn the freedom of this Nordic city,
Its green oxidised roofs and gulping gargoyles.
The English bookshop has next month's Penguins,
But I'm learning new words: *smörgåsbord*, *pilsner*, *duvet*.

On a pleasure boat cruising the blue canals,
An olive-skinned boy my age is collecting fares:
Youthful outsiders, we exchange complicit smiles.
Lights dance in the water by the floating tattooist.

Dinner tonight in the rooftop restaurant
Where an elderly pianist, Viennese and dapper,
Plays lollipops spiked with melancholia.
Old Europe's sadness drifts on the darkened sea.

Knole

The Sackvilles were mostly mad.
This book blames a 'rogue gene' for
that 'slow reclusive despair'
which drove them out of their minds.

Knole was, according to Burke,
'a pleasant habitation …
a grand repository':
oppressive clutter, more like.

But I remember the park
from winter afternoon runs:
setting off close to the gates,
rapidly losing the pack,

veering away to the right.
Distant scatter of antlers;
leafmould, twigs snapping, creatures
scuttling; not a soul in sight.

Along the wall of the house,
downhill back to the valley:
the runner's stumbling rhythm
leading to poems like this.

The Gardener

She starts almost from scratch. The garden sleeps,
Wrapped in a fallow blanket of neglect.
Rhubarb and horseradish silently erupt;
A long pale wound of birch-bark peels and weeps.

Experience will mend her early errors –
The rockery wall, the crazy-paving terrace
And fads for floribunda roses, dahlias –
Until this heavy acre holds no terrors.

The Flower Show awards her every trophy
(She likes the praise but hates the polishing).
There's fruit enough for eating and preserving;
Her kitchen garden yields unrationed plenty.

The child, who thinks his tricycle a bus,
Selects a tree-stump for its terminus.

1958

A reclamation job, this garden: planned
Through long Edwardian summers, gone to seed;
The children and the grandchildren of weed
Have colonised it as their promised land.

Slowly, outlines reappear: the rockery
Tumbles down to an overshadowed pond;
Apple and plum trees screen steep fields beyond;
Her cricket team of poplars lines the boundary.

Now terraced lawns sport freshly-printed stripes;
Pots and parterres wear their autumn shades;
And later, when the worst of winter fades,
The dell fills up with snowdrops, aconites.

Cycling along the drive, her son's at ease,
Blessed with confetti from the cherry trees.

1964

This garden's ready-made: another hill
Climbs to a Kentish oasthouse, while below
Walled steps and grassy terraces fall to
An ancient cottage named after its well.

With middle age comes order, and a diary:
She notes the sowing, planting, potting-on.
Dust carrots with soot. Give beans a lime solution.
Camellia buds are stripped or dropped: too dry.

Prune and shape Miss Jessup's Upright: April.
Divide and plant hepatica (two survived).
All the Patchwork Rarities annuals germinated.
Plant Wedding Day rambler by the Bramley apple.

The lanky boy, hunched over handlebars,
Pedals down the road, dreaming of cars.

1989

She starts again from scratch: a grassy mess.
By late November: *Garden rotovated,*
Paths and paving laid and pond constructed.
Here she creates her structured wilderness:

Shrubs and herbs; a fig tree by the wall;
Silver Jerusalem sage against red berberis;
Grey dappled light of sorbus; purple clematis.
Two drunken Irish yews stand sentinel.

The shadows lengthen. First her husband dies,
Then memory falters, joints become arthritic:
To spade and fork she adds a walking-stick.
Yet still she tends and prunes; the garden thrives.

She wills her own green burial: she knows
That what we plant outlives us, and outgrows.

In Sudbourne Wood

New season's sun: slant light of Aquarius;
Sky-blue shining puddles after days of rain;
Last year's bracken like shattered basketwork;
A sliced-off line of pallid-shanked Scots pines.

On the verge, a fallen bough with a dog's head
Stares up at me from among the alexanders.
A blackbird clacks and flaps at whatever has fired
His tiny anger. I remember the terrible summer.

These are calm days: the damage done repaired,
The account closed, a time to take stock slowly.
In the mid-afternoon distance, mist has gathered
Where the little church is snuggled in its valley.

Notes

The following poems, hitherto uncollected, appear here for the first time in book form: 'A Black Cat in July'; 'Solstice'; 'For My Ancestors'; 'The Window'; 'After Marriage'; '"Autumn is the curse of English poetry"'; 'A Midsummer Letter to Peter Thornton'; 'In a Cold Season'; 'A Late Summer Letter to Alec Chasemore'; 'Changing Trains'; 'Going Downhill'; 'Sleeper'; 'Raw'; 'For Andrew Mackinlay Esq, MP'.

A Black Cat in July. The cat was called Sooty; he lived at Oast Hill Farm, Sundridge, Kent.

Wickham Market. Written while staying in Aldeburgh during the summer between school and university. I'd like to claim that the (mostly half-) rhyming couplets were borrowed from Suffolk's great poet, George Crabbe, but they owe more to Thom Gunn.

Five Leaves Left. The reminder 'You have five leaves left' used to appear in packets of Rizla cigarette papers; in 1969, two years after this poem was written, Nick Drake entitled his first LP *Five Leaves Left*.

'Autumn is the curse of English poetry.' Said by K.W. Gransden, who was one of the judges at my interview for the 1968–9 Eric Gregory Award.

Wood Farm. A derelict farmhouse, subsequently restored, at Upper Billingford, Norfolk.

The Ruined Garden. At Toys Hill, Kent.

Distons Lane. In Chipping Norton, where I lived for eighteen months in 1970–1.

Period Three. This poem seems a bit unjust to Wordsworth; the set text was, perversely, the 1850 rather than the 1805 text of *The Prelude*.

Afternoon Dawn. The italicised words are from Gabriel García Márquez's *One Hundred Years of Solitude*.

For You. The deliberately unspecified 'You' in this sequence addresses several different people.

A Cooling Universe. The title is adapted from a phrase – 'a vacant universe and a cooling world' – in Graham Greene's *The Power and the Glory*. Matthew Desmond, whom I had met (but not taught) at Kimbolton School, was killed in a car accident in August 1975; this 'Hungarian' sequence of fifteen linked sonnets includes allusions to poems, books and music associated with him.

The Black Bechstein. The initials are those of my piano teacher, George Tester.

Stages. This sequence of poems was prompted by productions of *Troilus and Cressida* and *Hamlet* which I directed while teaching at St Christopher School, Letchworth.

Hawker at Morwenstow. In writing this poem, I was deeply indebted to Piers Brendon's book *Hawker of Morwenstow: Portrait of a Victorian Eccentric*.

Crabbe at Aldeburgh. The quotations are from *The Life of George Crabbe by His Son*.

The Noble Truce. Fulke Greville, in *Caelica* XLV, describes absence as 'the noble truce'.

In Arden: Cambridge, 1982. Phoebus Car was a summer travelling theatre group based at St Christopher School, Letchworth.

Studies. Each numbered stanza describes a different study-like room; in the second, the italicised '*Seniors*' are cigarettes.

Outside. This poem appears here as it was first published in the *Critical Quarterly*, Autumn 1986; the subject is imaginary but based on a childhood recollection of the Norfolk Broads. In my 1991 collection *True Colours*, I retitled it as 'An Alternative Ending' and added a dedication to my friend Ian Sizeland, whose family came from Norfolk.

The original version can't, alas, be dedicated to someone I hadn't yet met; but I hope this note makes some amends for that omission.

Poet and Pheasant, Totleigh Barton. Totleigh Barton is the Arvon Foundation's centre in North Devon.

The Stones on Thorpeness Beach. The starting-point of this poem is a painting by Guy Gladwell called *Thorpeness Dawn.*

Borodins and Vodka. The Borodin String Quartet was in residence at Aldeburgh in the early 1990s.

A Virus. The initials mentioned in the opening line are HIV.

Moving House. A dream-poem, in which the house, not its owner, is moving.

For Music. The poem (like, in this respect only, *Finnegans Wake*) is a loop: the rhyme scheme of the final stanza is completed by returning to the first.

Outing. The form is borrowed from Anthony Thwaite's 'On Consulting *Contemporary Poets of the English Language*'.

Yaxley. 'Freddie' is Sir Frederick Ashton; my grandmother, Lily Lloyd, was his housekeeper. Both also appear in 'My Chelsea' (p. 163).

After the Tempest. The speaker is Prospero.

Compost. Roy Fuller thought himself 'quite good material for compost' in 'Ludicrous Reflections', to be found in *From the Joke Shop.*

Hundred River. Adam Johnson died in May 1993.

The Picture of the Mind. The title is from Wordsworth, in *Tintern Abbey*: 'The picture of the mind revives again.'

The Boy on the Bus. This poem is spoken, or rather thought, by Hasib Hussain, Tavistock Square, 7 July 2005.

The Journal of Lily Lloyd. This preserves as closely as possible the vocabulary of my grandmother's original notebook, adapted and rearranged into eleven-syllable lines.

A Huntingdonshire Elegy. I borrowed the form and title, with the author's permission, from John Greening's *Huntingdonshire Elegies.* This poem alludes to 'Afternoon Dawn' (p. 28) and 'At the Edge' (p. 50). Rod Shand's remains were found in Lighthouse Park, Vancouver, in April 2011, a year after he disappeared.

Blackborough Park. This is, of course, a fiction. The park doesn't exist, although there is a Blackborough Road between Reigate and Redhill; this used to puzzle me when I was a child, since the place to which it seemed to refer couldn't be found.

Strand, 1923. The photograph is in *Literary Landscapes of the British Isles,* by David Daiches.

Louis Takes a Break. This is about Louis Armstrong's first recorded solo, in 'Chimes Blues' by King Oliver's Creole Jazz Band (7 April 1923).

Knole. The opening lines refer to *Inheritance: The Story of Knole and the Sackvilles,* by Robert Sackville-West.

The Gardener. My mother's four gardens were at Rowbarns Cottage, Leigh, Surrey; Clears House, Reigate, Surrey; The Well Cottage, Sundridge, Kent; and Castle Close, Orford, Suffolk.

The author would like to thank Grant Shipcott, for typesetting this book so handsomely in Caslon, and Adam Oliver, for his invaluable help with the proofs.

Index of First Lines

Index of Titles